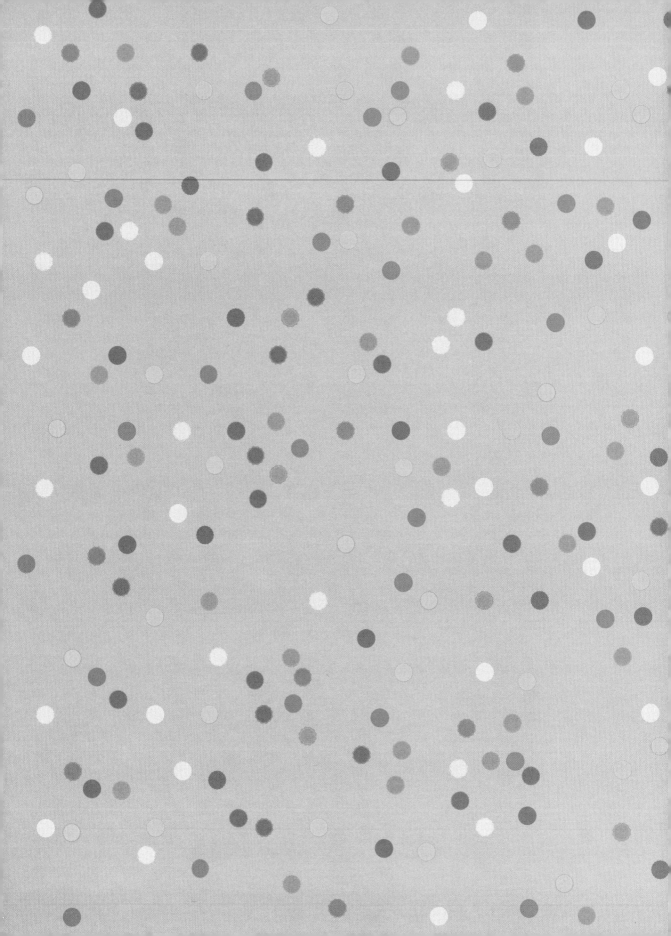

Let's Party

Unique kids' birthday party ideas

For my father – creative, playful and full of enthusiasm for new endeavours – who died while I was writing this book, and for my children – such sensitive, creative little souls – who made the hard slog worthwhile.

Martine Lleonart

Let's Party

Unique kids' birthday party ideas

hardie grant books

contents

introduction

Birthday parties seemed so simple when I was a kid: a handful of friends, a plate of cookies, pass the parcel and a slice of cake wrapped in a paper napkin to take home at the end. Sometimes we went to the circus, or a movie, but most often the party was at a friend's house.

The last two decades have seen the rise of the outsourced party. Why would you have a party at home if you could go to the latest rock climbing karaoke venue? But – here's the thing – children's birthday parties are not a competitive sport. Children actually love going to each other's homes: seeing a friend's bedroom for the first time, meeting their pets, trying out their toys. It gives them a chance to see their friends outside of the school context; as individuals with homes and families, and unique ways of doing things.

Another benefit of a home party is that you get to avoid the disposable plastic plates and cups, and use what you have in your cupboards. You can also reuse objects you have around the house as decorations, go to the opportunity (thrift) shop for props, raid your neighbour's garden for flowers, and collect fallen leaves and cones to fashion craft activities for the kids.

Having a party at home doesn't mean you have to do everything yourself, but it does allow you to be yourself. Work out what you want and have the time to do, and what you can outsource. If you're booking a play centre you might still like to make the cake or the party bags. Focus your efforts where you think they'll be best spent and don't feel that you have to do everything.

There are plenty of suggestions in this book for games and activities to keep kids busy, but don't schedule events so tightly that the kids can't improvise and make their own fun. Let them crawl under the table and pretend to be dogs if that's what they want to do; let them get muddy and dirty and climb trees and eat too much. It's in the unguarded, unscripted moments that they'll create lasting memories.

the guest list

When compiling your guest list, it's useful to remind yourself who the party is for. I know – it seems like a no-brainer, but it's easy to lose sight of the big picture.

If you're throwing a party for a one- or two-year-old, chances are your guest list is going to comprise mainly of adult family and close friends. You can still decorate and cater to your heart's content, but you probably don't need to go all out on games and activities unless you have lots of little cousins coming along.

From the ages of around three to five, as a general rule of thumb, the number of guests should equal roughly the age of the child. That is, if the child is turning four, then four or five special friends is just about right. This is, of course, entirely dependent on your child's temperament – some little children hate crowds and will have a much better time with three special friends, others would be happy with the whole kindergarten (preschool) class.

For younger children you might like to encourage the parents to stay. Have a 'parent station' set up in the kitchen with coffee, a selection of teas and everything they will need to make themselves a cuppa and a plate of something to nibble on.

Once children start primary (elementary) school there seems to be a never-ending cycle of birthday parties, particularly in the first two to three grades. It's not uncommon for some prep (kindergarten) kids to invite the whole class. Unless you a) are hiring out a play centre, b) live in a mansion with attendant servants, or c) love extreme sports, I would recommend limiting numbers for an at-home party to no more than 14 children. Personally, I've found anywhere between eight and 12 guests is a good number.

Once kids reach middle to upper primary, parties tend to get smaller again. Your child might prefer a few special friends for a sleepover rather than a big party.

Lastly, whatever age your child, if they have an absolute bestest, best, *best* friend, make sure they will be able to come on the day (or change the day so they can!).

invitations

As well as the date, start and finish times, venue and RSVP date (giving your mobile number *and* email address), the invitation should state how old the child is turning and ask for parents to alert you to any food allergies their child has.

I recommend sending out invitations around three weeks to a month before the big day. This should give people plenty of notice to schedule the party into their calendars.

A little decorum in handing out invitations can also go a long way. We've all seen it: the child in the playground handing out invitations to their super-duper special party, oblivious to the teary-looking kid who didn't get invited. I recommend emailing or texting the invitation (you can find the phone numbers on the class list handed out at the start of the year), then following up with a paper copy. For kindergarten children and younger school-age children, pop the invitation directly into the invited child's pigeonhole, or better still, give it to the parent at drop-off or pick-up. This will give you an early heads-up as to whether the children are likely to be attending or not.

Now, you emailed the invitation, you followed up with a paper copy for the fridge, but will they RSVP? Managing RSVPs can be a fraught process. It shouldn't be. Set the RSVP date for 10 days before the party. This will give you enough time to chase people and work out the catering. On the RSVP date, email or text (with the invite attached) all the outstanding people to RSVP. Keep it low key: something along the lines of 'Just checking in with you to see if Walter Jnr can make it to Oscar's party on the 16th?' If you don't hear back from them in 24 hours assume they are not coming.

timing

For younger children, limit parties to around 1½ hours. This breaks down roughly as:

- 15 minutes settling in and waiting for everyone to arrive (now is your chance to show them where the toilet is)
- 35 minutes playing games and activities
- 20 minutes for food
- 5 minutes for a quick run around while you tidy up the table before …
- 15 minutes for cake.

Once children reach around six to eight years you can increase to two hours. More complex activities and games will add on the extra time.

food & cake

food

How much effort you want to put into preparing the party food will depend on the age and number of your guests. For a big crowd, keep it as simple as possible and prepare as much in advance as you can. Toddlers will be happy with finger food. Anything bright and colourful will also be a hit. For older children you can really go to town with the themed party food.

The foods I've suggested in each party are specific to that theme but are not the whole picture. Add in whatever favourites your child has: pizza, meat pies, fries, hot dogs. A fruit platter is always a crowd pleaser and in summer a sushi platter is a nice cool treat.

cake

Even if you've never baked a cake before you can still put together an impressive birthday cake. Many major supermarkets sell plain cakes that you can decorate yourself. Keep it simple: whipped cream, jam, fresh strawberries. You can't go wrong. In cake supply stores you can even buy pre-made buttercream icing and there are lots of ready-made decorations available too.

As well as the individual cakes suggested for each party, there are recipes and loads of tips at the back of this book (pages 204-215).

allergies

If you have children coming to the party who have allergies (particularly the life-threatening variety), give that food a wide berth. It will make it much easier on everyone and you can relax and not worry about Junior getting into the nut bowl.

Dealing with dairy, egg or gluten intolerance is much easier these days with many products, including sweets, chocolate and marshmallows, catering to these allergies (packaging is usually well labelled). Please be aware that there is a difference between being gluten-intolerant and having coeliac disease. Even traces of gluten can be dangerous for kids with coeliac – if in doubt, check with the parents.

party favours

The party favours I've suggested in this book are theme-specific, but there are also many ideas you can take and modify for your own themes. Mix and match as you please. If you're short of time or don't want to put the effort into this aspect of the party, load up the bags with shop-bought goodies.

I'd recommend making up a few extra party bags in case of doe-eyed siblings showing up at the end of the party – clearly I'm a sucker. The 'extra' party bags don't have to be the same: pop in a few stickers, a funny eraser or two, and a couple of sweets and they'll be happy.

I like to have the party bags on display. When I say display, it's code for 'look but don't touch'. Pinning the party bags onto a wall (i.e. out of reach) using string and pegs is a really simple way to display them.

For toddlers, handles on the party bags are great – they love to carry things around with them.

party day

back-up plans

If you're planning on having the party at a park or in your backyard, have a back-up plan in mind. Will you be able to accommodate everyone in your home if it rains? Consider having a movie lined up as Plan B, or some simple party games ready to go.

And if the worst-case scenario does happen and your child wakes up on the morning of the party with gastro, concede defeat early. Cancel and reschedule for a couple of weeks' time. Yes, the birthday child will be shattered, but you can still make the day special by setting up a cosy nook to watch a favourite movie with your child.

contact list

The day before the party, print out a list of all the names of the children attending, along with their parents' names and contact phone numbers. When Ethel starts vomiting up frankfurters or Carson breaks his arm kung-fu fighting with a giant inflatable tyrannosaurus rex, you don't want to be scrambling around trying to retrieve phone numbers from your mobile phone – especially if it needed charging last night and you forgot to plug it in.

presents

Before the party you might want to prep your child on the graceful acceptance of presents. Most of us aren't born with exceptional manners and the occasional priming doesn't go astray – it also avoids the scenario of having your child grab a present and screech, 'It's not very big!' For younger children, I'd recommend having a designated area set up for presents and a rule about not opening them until after the party.

pets

If you have pets make sure they are out of harm's way on the day of the party. Some children are very scared of dogs (and cats) if they aren't used to them. I'd suggest asking a neighbour or friend to take the dog for the duration of the party, or at least make sure it is confined to a restricted area.

thank-you notes

You can get your child to contribute (in an age-appropriate way) to sending thank-yous but don't force them to painstakingly write out individual thank-you notes. You could ask them to draw a picture of the party and then email the picture to the parents of the attending children. You might also want to share some photos from the party with parents. Another idea is to have the phone ready when your child opens each present so that you can take a snap and send it to the gift-giver's parents.

rainbow

presenting nature's ultimate
party trick: the rainbow

This has to be one of my
favourite party themes. Everyone
loves rainbows. They are
undeniably awesome.

decorations

I recommend keeping some of the decorations for this party at toddler height, so they can really get in amongst it.

rainbow smash

- balloons
- blue and white tissue paper pompoms
- tissue paper honeycomb balls
- helium balloons
- feature pieces, such as rainbow forest saplings (below)

You will need colourful balloons of different sizes, white tissue paper pompoms to hang on the wall as decorative clouds (you need some clouds to generate the rainbows), tissue paper honeycomb balls in various sizes for the ground level (they are more robust than the pompoms), a few oversized helium balloons and just a couple of feature pieces, such as a cloud mobile and rainbow saplings – ta da, an indoor rainbow!

rainbow forest saplings

- sticks
- little felt balls in various colours
- hot glue gun
- vase

Is there anything a felt ball can't do? I think not. And that's why I hot-glued these little balls onto some bare branches and made *an actual real life rainbow tree* (see the image on page 19).

cloudy with a chance of rainbows

- white card or white felt
- white embroidery thread
- embroidery needle
- blue felt balls (available at good craft stores) or you could make little blue pompoms
- small tree branch (or a large stick – depends how you look at it)

Make two clouds – draw one big and one itty-bitty one on white card (you can use the template on page 218) or make up some little cloud friends in white felt (see page 25). Thread felt balls on different lengths of thread using a needle, then tie a big knot at the end of each thread so the felt balls don't slip off. Glue or sew your dangly felt balls to the clouds as rain drops. Tie your clouds to a stick and you have a cloud mobile (see the image on page 18).

activities

additional ideas

pin the tail on the unicorn (see page 42); make a Fruit Loop necklace (page 154); cut cloud shapes from white card for a game of musical clouds (see page 118)

rainbow dancing ribbons

- ribbons in rainbow colours
- wooden curtain rings

Tie the ribbons to the curtain rings (or help the children do it), hand them around, add some music and get your dance moves on.

rainbow celery fish painting

- white paper
- black marker pen
- lots of celery sticks
- red, orange, yellow, green, blue and purple non-toxic paints in little tubs

Draw fish shapes onto paper and have them ready to go. Pre-cut the celery (the kids will use the stalks to paint scales on the fish) and store in a container in the refrigerator.

Add paint and small children.

balloon in a basket

- laundry basket
- assortment of coloured pool noodles
- balloons in various colours

Place the basket in the middle of the room, hand out the pool noodles and see who can score a goal by hitting their balloon into the basket (no hands allowed).

rainbow treasure hunt

There are infinite options for rainbow treasure, but here are some suggestions:

- red balls or a red bowl full of tomatoes
- orange play blocks or oranges
- bananas or a yellow bucket
- green apples or a green blanket
- blue tissue paper pompoms or a blue cushion
- purple crayons or a purple soft toy

You'll need plenty of colourful things dotted around for the children to find (use my suggestions or come up with your own colourful treasure).

You could tape a big poster with little pictures of the items to the wall so that everyone can see what they're looking for.

food

rainbow fairy bread

- thin-sliced, soft white bread
- butter
- sprinkles

Trim the crusts off the bread, then spread the slices with butter and cover with sprinkles. Cut each bread slice in half and roll them up like a Swiss roll.

fruit kebabs

- kebab sticks
- raspberries, oranges, pineapple, kiwi fruit, blueberries, red grapes

Thread fruit pieces onto kebab sticks to create a rainbow effect. So pretty. Remember to cut off the sharp ends of the kebab sticks. You could layer these fruits in a clear plastic cup if you're worried about the sticks being too tricky for the littlies.

strawberry rainbows

- strawberries
- white chocolate, melted
- sprinkles

Wash and pat dry strawberries. Dip them in melted white chocolate and then dip them in sprinkles.

rainbow jelly

- 600 ml (20½ fl oz/2¼ cups) cream, for whipping
- 10 tall clear cups
- 6 packets of jelly (Jell-O) crystals, to match the colours of the rainbow

Makes 10 serves

These cups will be a big hit. They are time consuming, but the other food options suggested here are super easy and quick.

To make the whipped cream, use an electric mixer on high speed to whisk the cream until soft peaks form. For your first colour add one cup of boiling water to one packet of jelly crystals and stir until dissolved. While hot, pour half this mixture into another bowl and whisk in half a cup of whipped cream. Pour the creamy layer into the bottoms of all the cups and allow to set in the refrigerator (around 20 minutes – it won't take as long as normal for the jelly to set because it is such a little amount). Meanwhile, keep your warm clear jelly sitting on the bench (you don't want it to set yet). When your first opaque layer has set, use a funnel to gently pour on the second layer. Back in the refrigerator it goes. Now repeat five more times with the other colours.

citrus rainbow lemonade

- lime, lemon, orange, ruby grapefruit, blood orange
- 1 litre (34 fl oz/4 cups) lemonade (lemon-lime soda) or soda water

Place slices of each fruit in a tall narrow jug or jar to make this pretty drink. Pour your choice of drink (water, lemonade ... vodka ... hang on, that comes later) onto the fruit and top with ice cubes. (The jar needs to be narrow so that the fruit stays where you put it and doesn't float around in the jug willy-nilly.)

cake

naked rainbow cake

Make the white cake recipe on page 210.

- half quantity of Swiss meringue buttercream (page 206)
- icing (confectioners') sugar, to dust

decoration
- cloud friends (page 25)
- coloured straws or plastic sticks

Serves 20

The rainbow cake has become very popular in recent years, and although it isn't the best-tasting cake around, it looks super impressive.

I'm partial to naked cakes, but especially in this instance – why cover up all those pretty colours? Add some clouds for extra dazzle.

When it's time to assemble the cake, place your first layer on the cake stand and pipe (I used a star tip) the buttercream around the centre of the cake. Don't go closer than a finger width to the edge (especially on the bottom layer) because the weight of the other layers will push the buttercream out to the edges. Add cake layers and buttercream until you get to the top. Now go back around the sides of the cake with the piping bag to make pretty piped edges.

Pop the whole thing back in the refrigerator to firm up the buttercream.

Before serving, dust the top of the cake with icing (confectioners') sugar and add some felt cloud friends (fix them onto thin straws or plastic sticks – cocktail swizzle sticks work well).

party favours

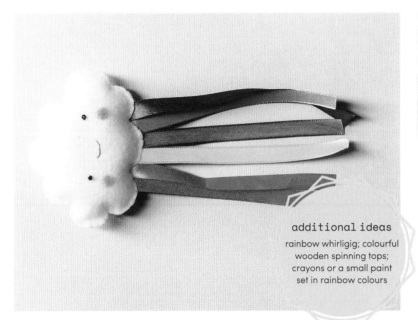

additional ideas
rainbow whirligig; colourful
wooden spinning tops;
crayons or a small paint
set in rainbow colours

rainbow favour bag

- white card
- marker pens
- ribbons in rainbow colours
- blue paper party bags
- glue
- small wooden pegs

These little favour bags are sweet and simple. Cut a cloud shape (see page 218) from white card, draw on a face and glue the rainbow ribbons to the bottom of the cloud. Now stick the cloud to the party bag, fill with goodies and close with a peg.

rainbow bracelets

- elastic thread or cord
- jelly beans
- large darning needle

Cut the elastic into pieces about 15 cm (6 in) long. Tie a knot about 2 cm (1 in) from one end of each piece of elastic. Using the darning needle, thread the elastic through the jelly beans, sliding them along. When you have enough for a bracelet tie the elastic ends together. You could also use mini felt balls in rainbow colours.

cloud friends

- white and pink felt
- black embroidery thread
- small black beads for eyes (only for the over-threes – use embroidery thread for smaller tots)
- hot glue gun
- ribbons in rainbow colours
- fixing pins
- stuffing

Take two layers of white felt and cut out two cloud shapes (use the template on page 218). Cut out tiny rounds from pink felt for the cheeks (you could use a holepunch for this).

Embroider or sew eyes and mouth onto one cloud piece. Use hot glue to stick the little pink cheeks on. Put the two cloud pieces together and pin the ribbons into place at the bottom of the cloud. Sew from one side of the ribbons all the way around to the other side using blanket stitch (there are excellent tutorials on embroidery stitches online if you need to brush up on your needlework knowledge). Stuff then sew the opening closed.

teddy bears' picnic

let your teddy bears get back to nature

This is a very adaptable little party because it's a picnic: you can pick it up and take it with you to the local park if you don't have a backyard. And remember, this is a strictly BYO bear affair, so remember to make some extra treats for the bears, too.

decorations

Since this is a teddy bears' picnic and most teddy bears are small in stature, keep the decorations for this party close to the ground. You'll need picnic rugs, cushions and a low table for the food.

the bears' retreat

- 2 or 3 large sticks or bamboo poles
- string
- tissue paper tassels (from party supply stores)

This is a cosy spot just for the children and their special guests. Push the sticks or poles very firmly into the ground. Run the string between the poles and hang paper tassels and other bear-friendly decorations from them. You could also suspend the decorations from a friendly tree.

bear ears

- needle and twine
- small coloured pompoms
- soft headbands

Using a needle, thread short pieces of twine through the bottom half of the pompoms, then tie two pompoms onto each headband for the children to wear as bear ears (see the image on page 31).

Instant cuteness!

follow the bear prints

- chalk

Use white chalk to draw bear footprints along the footpath outside your house or apartment block, heading to the front door (use the illustration above for inspiration).

activities

hand-print bear

- bear faces: brown card, black marker pen, glue
- paint in a shallow dish
- white A4 paper
- glue
- washing-up tub for messy paws

Pre-prepare bear faces for the party by cutting out a large round card shape for the face and two smaller ones for the ears. Using the image opposite as a guide, glue the three pieces together and draw on eyes and a muzzle.

Each child takes a turn at dipping their hand into the paint and pressing it onto a sheet of paper to make a bear's body. Help the children to stick a bear face in position. Remember to write the child's name on their artwork. Allow to dry – the bear prints should be ready to take home by the end of the party.

teddy parachute toss

- play parachute (or an old sheet will do the trick)
- lots of teddies

Get the kids to place the teddies in the middle of the parachute, then ask them to stand around the perimeter of the parachute: all count '1, 2, 3, lift!' and watch them fly. See how many bears are safely caught!

pass the parcel

- lots of wrapping paper
- little packets of Tiny Teddies (Teddy Grahams)
- little packets of Gummy Bears

Prepare the parcel, wrapping alternate layers with packets of Tiny Teddies and packets of Gummy Bears (the idea being that the children can't get their mitts on the actual sweets until a parent helps them open the packets).

The children sit in a circle on the floor and pass the parcel around the circle while music plays in the background. When the music stops (an adult should be in charge of the music to ensure it stops at the right time), the child holding the parcel gets to open a layer of the parcel, revealing a small gift. Keep going until every child has had a turn at opening a layer, leaving the very last layer for the birthday child.

teddy bear song

Don teddy bear ears (see page 28), get out the teddies and get active for this song.

Teddy bear, teddy bear,
Turn around!
Teddy bear, teddy bear,
Touch the ground!
Teddy bear, teddy bear,
Jump up high!
Teddy bear, teddy bear,
Touch the sky!

Teddy bear, teddy bear,
Bend down low!
Teddy bear, teddy bear,
Touch your toes!
Teddy bear, teddy bear,
Turn out the light!
Teddy bear, teddy bear,
Say good night!

additional ideas

pin the tail on the bear (see page 42); beehive piñata; musical cushions (see page 118)

food

For older children, you could serve up the bear buns from the Woodland Animals party (page 120), but for younger children it's probably best to stick to simpler fare.

bear sandwiches

- thin-sliced bread
- bear-shaped cookie cutter or mould
- fillings of your choice

All you need is a bear-shaped cookie cutter to make simple crustless bear sandwiches.

teddy fruit cups

- cupcake cases
- card in various colours
- glue
- black marker pen
- blueberries
- strawberries

Turn cupcake cases into friendly little bears. Cut a round face, two small round ears and a little oval-shaped snout from card. Using the image opposite as a guide, assemble the bear with glue and draw on eyes and a muzzle. Attach to the cases and fill them with blueberries and cut-up strawberries.

teddy racing cars

- small amount of melted dark chocolate
- Tiny Teddies (Teddy Grahams) with their legs cut off
- Tim Tams or any chocolate-covered rectangular biscuit (cookie)
- Smarties (M&Ms)

Use the melted chocolate to stick the teddies on the chocolate biscuit 'cars'. Using more melted chocolate, add Smarties to the side of the biscuits for the wheels and stick halved Smarties on top of the biscuits as the steering wheel.

old-school biscuits

- 2 packets of teddy-shaped biscuits (chocolate and plain)
- edible sugar flowers (from the cake aisle at the supermarket)
- small amount of melted chocolate

You could make your own chocolate teddy-shaped biscuits, but the packet ones are so good you really can't go past them. They scream birthday party. Dazzle the partygoers by mixing plain and chocolate-flavoured bears on the same plate. Use melted chocolate to glue on sugar flowers to make girl bears. Fancy.

bear bottles

- coloured card
- black marker pen
- glue
- double-sided sticky tape
- small milk bottles
- coloured twine
- milk or juice

Make bear faces from card – see the instructions for teddy fruit cups above – and use tape to stick them to milk bottles (you can buy bottles with lids and in-built straws to avoid spillages; alternatively, you could get clear plastic cups with lids and straws if you are worried about breakages). Tie a short piece of pretty twine around the neck of the bottle in a bow.

Fill with bear juice of your choice.

cake

Neapolitan bear cake

This sweet bear cake is based on a design by Lyndsay Sung from Coco Cake Land.

Make double the quantity of the basic butter cake on page 213, then follow instructions here for colouring the three layers.

- raspberry food flavouring
- 2 tablespoons Dutch (unsweetened) cocoa powder

icing & decoration

- white and black fondant (see page 207)
- black gel paste food colour
- teal gel paste food colour
- one quantity Swiss meringue buttercream (page 206)
- violet gel paste food colour
- grass piping nozzle for the bear's fur

Serves 16–20

Use white fondant for the bear's muzzle and colour some fondant with teal food colour for the ears, as pictured here – or improvise. Use black fondant for the bear's facial features. Now for the cake.

Grease and line three round cake tins (20 cm x 5 cm/8 in x 2 in) with baking paper (parchment). Make double the butter cake batter and divide equally into three separate bowls. Add raspberry food flavouring to one batch and two tablespoons of cocoa to another batch (the third batch is the vanilla).

Pour the batter into the three prepared cake tins. Bake for approximately 35–40 minutes. They're ready when a skewer inserted into the middle comes out clean. Remove from the oven and allow to cool for 10 minutes before turning onto cooling racks. When cool carefully cut the rounded top off the cakes with a long serrated knife.

Make a batch of Swiss meringue buttercream and take the colour back to white by adding violet gel paste food colour (see page 206). Don't add the teal colour yet. Place the cocoa cake layer on the cake board/stand. Use a spatula to smear on a layer of white buttercream. Place the vanilla cake layer and again top with buttercream. Top with the raspberry cake.

You should have a lot of buttercream left over. Now add teal gel paste food colour a little at a time until you get a shade you're happy with. Prepare the cake with a crumb coat (page 204).

If you haven't used a grass nozzle before have a practice first. It's quite easy once you get the hang of it. You need to position the nozzle so it's just touching the cake. Squeeze a little, then lift. Now, you've got a lot of fur to make and I can pretty much guarantee you're going to get a sore wrist. I suggest doing the sides first, then popping the cake in the refrigerator while you have a break and contemplate why you got yourself into this. When you're ready, finish the top with the grass tip and chill again for 30 minutes. Position the bear's facial features by lightly placing them on top of the buttercream fur.

Keep the cake in an open cake box (don't shut the lid or the fondant will go soggy) or just on a cake stand in a cool place until ready to serve. (It's fine to sit out of the refrigerator like this for up to a day.)

party favours

teddy bear favour bags

- blue paper party bags
- white card
- black marker pen
- glue
- small wooden pegs

Fold the top quarter of the party bags over. Cut out bear ears and a muzzle from white card. Draw the bear's mouth and nose on the muzzle, then glue the ears onto the top outer edge of the paper bags. Position the muzzle in the middle of the bag and glue in place. Draw on eyes, fill the bags and close them with a wooden peg.

These bags are perfect for the hang-and-display treatment – safe from little hands until they are ready to be handed out.

teddy bear crayons

- old broken crayons
- silicone teddy bear mould

Preheat the oven to 100°C (200°F) and line a tray with baking paper (parchment). Chop up the crayons into little pieces and arrange in the mould. Pile the pieces up a little higher than the top of the mould because when the crayons melt they will take up less space. Put the mould on the tray and cook for 12–15 minutes. Remove from the oven and let the bear crayons cool completely before removing them from the mould.

sleepy teddy bear

- small tin or box for the bed
- teddy-shaped cookie cutter
- brown felt
- light brown felt
- dark brown embroidery thread
- stuffing
- scraps of felt or pretty material

Measure a small tin or box to make sure your teddy will fit nicely in the bed. Now use a teddy-shaped cookie cutter to trace and cut two bear shapes from brown felt. Cut one small oval from the light brown felt for the muzzle.

Use the dark brown embroidery thread to sew a nose and mouth onto the muzzle. Sew the muzzle onto the face of one of the bear shapes. Sew on eyes using dark brown embroidery thread in a French knot (there are excellent tutorials on all types of embroidery stitches online if you need to brush up on your needlework knowledge). Layer the two bear shapes, then, beginning at one arm, sew the whole way around the teddy using blanket stitch. Remember to leave a small gap so that you can fill the teddy with stuffing before you sew it all up.

Make a comfy bed for your teddy by creating a sheet and pillow from pretty fabric scraps.

additional ideas
buzzy bee bubbles
(wrap yellow bubble bottles
with thin lines of black tape
and attach pipe cleaner
antennae); a strawberry
friend (page 149); wooden
spinning tops

bunny love

so cute, so fluffy, it must be a bunny

If you're after a simple and sweet party theme for your little one you can't go past a bunny party.

decorations

Lots of paper flowers and simple party games make this party adaptable to any favourite animal your child may have.

paper flowers

- card in several colours
- hot glue gun
- green card, for leaves
- tissue paper

Paper flowers are simple to make and very adaptable. You can make all sorts of different types of flowers using crepe or tissue paper, but I'm sticking to simple card here. You can make pointed petals, rounded petals, double-pointed petals. You can have a single layer of petals or make multiple layers.

For these flowers, choose your petal colours then cut four large petal shapes, four medium petal shapes and four small petal shapes (see the template on page 218). Trace a large circle (a dinner plate is good) on card and cut out: this will be your base. Cut a multi-pronged star shape for the stamen (see page 218; I used yellow card, but you can use any colour you like).

Cut a slit in the base of all the petals following the template on page 218 to split the bottom of your petal into two sides. Now fold the right side over the left side and fix it in place with hot glue to give the petals shape. Arrange the four largest petals around your base and glue in place. Position the medium petals inside the larger petals and glue, then do the small petals.

Poke a hole in the middle of the stamen. Next, concertina fold an 8 x 8 cm (3 x 3 in) length of tissue paper, twist one end of it and cut along the centre of the piece from the other end, to about two-thirds of the way down. Poke the twisted end through the hole in the stamen to secure. Hot glue the stamen to the centre of the flower and loosen up the tissue paper to create the pollen.

You can cut out green card leaves and add them to some of the flowers – just glue the leaves onto the back of the flower base. There are heaps of great flower templates online if you feel like experimenting.

adopt-a-bunny centre

- basket
- paper flowers (see above)
- felt bunnies (page 48)

Decorate a basket with some little paper flowers and place a batch of felt bunnies inside for adoption – your little guests can take their bunny friend home at the end of the party.

bunny food cones & bunny milk bottles

- white and pink card
- holepunch
- glue
- black marker pen
- coloured card or paper for cones
- double-sided sticky tape
- milk bottles

Make little bunny faces from white and pink card (see the image on page 45) – cut out a shape for the bunny head and the insides of bunny's ears, and punch out two small pink cheeks. Assemble the face, then draw on the eyes, nose and mouth with black marker pen.

For the food cones, make a simple cone by cutting a 14 cm (5½ in) diameter semi-circle from card (use a compass), bring the straight sides together, overlap them to your desired shape and tape them together. Stick the bunny faces on.

For the milk bottles, tape bunny faces to the bottles (if you're worried about spillages, use little milk bottles with lids and in-built straws).

activities

pin the tail on the bunny

- grey felt
- fluffy white pompom
- strip of stick-on Velcro
- fabric for the blindfold
- corkboard (optional)

No bunny party would be complete without pinning the tail on the bunny.

Cut a bunny shape from felt and mount it on the wall (you could also pin or glue it onto a corkboard). Stick a pompom tail onto a piece of Velcro – use the hook part of the Velcro strip, as it will easily attach to felt.

Now blindfold your little guests and hand them the pompom to pin the tail.

decorate bunny ears

- card
- elastic thread
- glitter
- sequins
- felt balls
- glue sticks
- marker pens

Prepare the activity by cutting bunny headbands from card in colours of your choice (use the image opposite as a guide) and attaching elastic thread to the sides – just poke two small holes into the card, thread the elastic through and tie knots.

Set up an activity table and provide lots of embellishments for the little bunnies to decorate their ears with. Sequins, glitter and felt balls are all good options to add some bunny bling!

bunny hop race

- old pillowcases, or some hessian (burlap) to make sacks
- pompoms
- glue or thread

Now that the bunnies have ears they'll be ready for a sack race. You can pick up some old pillowcases from the op shop (thrift store) or make sacks from hessian. Just sew or glue on a pompom for a tail. Hippity-hop.

Line the kids up for a race of all against all, or for older kids make it a bunny relay (you could even place some obstacles for the bunnies to hop around for extra fun).

additional ideas
cut large carrot shapes
from orange card for the
children to sit on for a game
of musical carrots (see
page 118); bunny bingo;
hide-and-seek bunny

food

carrot sticks & dip

- carrots, peeled and cut into thin sticks
- dip of your choice
- pretzels

Essential munching for bunnies of all ages. Bunnies are quite fond of pretzels, too.

bunny sandwiches

- thin-sliced bread
- bunny-shaped cookie cutter or mould
- fillings of your choice

Use a bunny cookie cutter to create yummy bunny sandwiches.

fruit waffle cones

- waffle cones
- fruit of your choice
- bunny food cones (page 40)

Fill waffle cones with berries and chopped fruit and then pop them into bunny food cones.

bunny poop & bunny tails

- chocolate-coated sultanas (raisins)
- Raffaello treats

Be sure to include chocolate-coated sultanas and Raffaello coconut treats on your food table for some bunny-themed sweets.

bunny milk

- milk
- flavouring (optional)
- bunny milk bottles (page 40)

Pour plain or flavoured milk into your bunny milk bottles.

cake

'bunnies in the garden' banana cake

- 125 g (4½ oz) unsalted butter, at room temperature
- 325 g (11½ oz/1½ cups) caster (superfine) sugar
- 250 g (9 oz/1⅔ cups) plain (all-purpose) flour
- 1 teaspoon bicarbonate of soda (baking soda)
- ½ teaspoon ground cinnamon
- ½ teaspoon ground ginger
- ¼ teaspoon vanilla extract
- 2 eggs, lightly whisked
- 1 cup mashed banana (about 3 bananas)
- 125 ml (4 fl oz/½ cup) buttermilk

lemon cream cheese icing

- 500 g (1 lb 2 oz) cream cheese, at room temperature
- 120 g (4½ oz) butter, unsalted, at room temperature
- 300 g (10½ oz/3 cups) icing (confectioners') sugar, sifted
- 1 teaspoon vanilla extract
- 1 teaspoon lemon zest

decorations

- small bunny figurines if you have them; alternatively, make bunnies from fondant (see page 207)
- 2 sticks (give them a good clean)
- mini flower garland (cardboard flowers, string, sticky tape; see page 40)

Serves 16

Preheat oven to 170°C (340°F). Grease and line the bottom and sides of a deep 20 cm (8 in) round cake tin.

Beat butter and sugar together in a large bowl until light and fluffy.

Sift together the dry ingredients.

In a separate bowl add the vanilla and eggs to the mashed banana.

Beat the banana mash into the butter and sugar. Stir in half the sifted dry ingredients, then half the buttermilk, then the remaining dry ingredients and remaining buttermilk.

Pour into the prepared cake tin and bake in a preheated oven for 55–70 minutes. It's done when a skewer inserted into the middle comes out clean.

Allow to cool for 10 minutes before turning out onto a cooling rack, then allow to cool completely before cutting the top off to make it nice and flat.

When you are ready to ice the cake, beat all the icing ingredients together. Taste and adjust as necessary.

It's important to start with a crumb coat (page 204) on this cake to achieve a lovely overall smooth finish. Collect some bunny friends and two sticks. Coat one end of each stick with some icing and put the sticks in the refrigerator for the icing to set. Apply a thick second layer of icing to the cake and pop your bunny friends into position. Refrigerate.

For the flower garland, create small versions of the paper flowers on page 40 and fix them to string using sticky tape.

Finish by poking the sticks into the cake and tying on the flower garland.

party favours

bunny favour bags

- white and pink card
- holepunch
- black marker pen
- hot glue gun
- hessian (burlap) bags
- needle and twine

These hessian bunny bags are easy to make: cut a face, tail and the inside of bunny's ears from card (use the image opposite as a guide) and make little pink cheeks using a holepunch. Assemble your bunny. Draw on eyes and a little nose and hot glue the face and tail to the hessian bag, then thread some twine through the top and tie a bow.

bunny sweets bags

- white and pink card
- holepunch
- black marker pen
- mini zip-lock plastic bags
- sweets of your choice
- double-sided sticky tape

Cut a trapezoid from card (see the image opposite) and add a bunny face and little card bunny ears and cheeks. Fill the bags with sweet treats and use tape to stick the bunny face to the top of the bag.

felt bunnies

- felt
- contrasting fabric
  (felt or any pretty fabric)
- embroidery thread for finishing edges
- stuffing
- fixing pins
- mini pompoms
- hot glue gun (optional)

These little bunnies are very simple.

Cut felt shapes from the template (page 216). Use blanket stitch to sew the arms, legs and ears together in pairs (there are excellent tutorials on embroidery stitches online if you need to brush up on your needlework knowledge). Put a little stuffing into the arms and legs (but not the ears). Add facial details to your bunny. Sew the tummy patch onto bunny's front, then pin the legs, arms and ears into position on bunny's body and sew with blanket stitch from one arm clockwise all the way around the body and to the ear closest to the arm you started at. Fill your bunny with stuffing and sew closed.

Hot glue on little pink cheeks and a pompom for the tail if you like. Ta da!

additional ideas
bunny origami (page 191);
tic-tac-toe (page 61);
felt acorns (page 125)

farm

moo baa la la la

Small children are fascinated by farm animals. Why is that? Do they intuitively know it's where lunch came from? I hope not. In any case, I love a farm party. If your budget permits, the farm can come to you. There are companies that will bring small petting zoos to your party and the children get the opportunity to bottle feed a lamb or hold a chick. But the kids will be equally happy with some traditional farm-themed games.

decorations

Dig out your gingham, grab a hay bale and convert your home into the farmhouse you've always wanted.

fabric strip garland

- fabric in 3 or 4 patterns
- broom stick
- string

Choose fabrics with a farm vibe (I used hessian [burlap], gingham, cow print and a floral). Cut or tear into strips of around 5 cm x 60 cm (2 in x 23 in). I did eight of each fabric. Fold them in half lengthways and tie them to a broom handle. Tie a piece of string to two points of the broom handle and hang it off a hook in the wall.

weather vane

- white, grey and red card
- black marker pen
- glue and sticky tape
- stick or skewer
- farm cupcakes (page 60)

Cut two squares from white card and four interconnected arrows from grey card – use the image opposite as a guide, or create your own design. Layer the two squares, then turn the top square by 45° and glue it onto the square below. Draw the four cardinal points into each corner of the top square and glue the arrows into the centre of the compass. Mount the compass onto contrasting coloured card (I used a red card multi-pronged star shape as my backdrop, but feel free to pick any background shape and colour you like). Next, cut out a rooster (use the template on page 221) and single arrow. Glue or tape the compass card, rooster and arrow to the stick and poke it into a farm cupcake.

farm flowers

- strips of hessian (burlap)
- mason jar
- gingham fabric or ribbon
- cottage flowers

Wrap strips of hessian around the jar and tie a gingham bow over it. Fill with cottage flowers.

activities

potato sack race

- potato sacks, or hessian (burlap)

If you can't find any old potato sacks, make some up with hessian. Don't make the sacks too big, as it's hard for smaller children to hold them up.

Make the race as easy or as complex as you like, depending on the age of the children. For extra fun, add in some obstacles such as hay bales that they have to jump around. Or have them make farm animal noises while they are racing. For instance, call out 'pig' and all the children have to start oinking, then change to donkey, cow and chicken.

duck pond

- large bucket or tub
- rubber duckies
- scoops or butterfly nets

Fill the tub with water, drop in the duckies and give the children a scoop or net to catch them.

egg & spoon race

- spoon for each child
- egg for each child

You can't have a farm party without a traditional egg and spoon race.

The kids can compete individually or, for older children, you could team them up for a relay – it gets tricky when they have to pass the spoon to the next person without dropping the egg.

I'll leave you to decide the big question: hard-boiled or raw?

additional ideas

the classic children's game duck, duck, goose; an egg hunt (fill plastic eggs with sweets or hide chocolate eggs); farm animal charades

food

strawberry pig bagels

- strawberries
- bagels
- cream cheese
- blueberries

Cut a slice of the strawberry widthways from the widest point of the strawberry. This will be the nose. Now cut the pointy end in two lengthways: these are the ears. Cut bagels in half and spread cream cheese on each side. Take the round piece of strawberry and place it across the bagel hole. Place a blueberry on top for nostrils. Pop two blueberries in place for the eyes and position the pointy ears. (You could blend the cream cheese with a few strawberries to create a pink face.)

farm-fresh fruit tubs

- 1 tablespoon honey
- 375 ml (12½ fl oz/1½ cups) plain yoghurt
- 750 g (1 lb 11 oz) fresh or frozen raspberries (or other fruit)
- 10 plastic or paper cups
- 10 popsicle sticks

Makes 10

Stir the honey through the yoghurt until well combined. Put a handful of fruit aside and blend the rest lightly using a hand blender. Only blend a little bit – you want to keep some chunky bits. Add about half a cup of the yoghurt mix to the berries and stir through.

Spoon the berry mash into the bottoms of the cups, fill to near the top with yoghurt, then squish down with a spoon to remove any air pockets. Or give it a little jiggle. Now poke your popsicle sticks in. Top with a few raspberry pieces. Into the freezer they go.

Once they are frozen, if they are stubborn to come out of their cosy containers run them under lukewarm water for a few seconds.

As an alternative to raspberries, use strawberries, bananas or blackberries.

milk fresh from the farm

- small milk bottles
- chocolate, melted
- sprinkles
- strips of hessian (burlap)
- strips of gingham
- straws

Dip the tops of glass milk bottles in melted chocolate, then into sprinkles and leave to set. Wrap the bottles with strips of hessian and then top with the gingham tied in a bow. Pour in the milk and add a straw to serve.

food

little chicks

- carrots, lightly steamed
- 10 eggs, hard-boiled and peeled
- currants

Makes 10

The carrots should be just a little tender – steam them enough to take out the crunch. Cut into rounds by slicing widthways. Now cut little spikes into each round to make the combs. Cut little triangles for the beaks. Cut the top third of the egg down the centre and poke in the comb and beak. Gently push the currants in place for the eyes. (If you want extra cuteness, use one large hen's egg and a dozen quail eggs to make a mother hen and her chicks.)

corn on the cob popcorn packs

- popcorn
- clear cellophane party bags
- twine
- green tissue paper

Place the popcorn in the party bags, twist then tie the bags' opening with twine to secure. Wrap green tissue paper around the corn bags – turn the bags upside down to hide the tied-up end in the green tissue paper and leave the bottom of the party bags exposed to look like the head of a cob of corn. Secure the tissue paper in place by tying more twine around the outside of your cobs. To access the popcorn, cut or tear open the party bags.

cake

Tahli's 'down on the farm' cupcakes

- 220 g (8 oz) unsalted butter
- 220 g (8 oz) chocolate
- 160 ml (5½ fl oz/⅔ cup) water
- 125 g (4½ oz/¾ cup) plain (all-purpose) flour
- 125 g (4½ oz/¾ cup) self-raising flour (or 125 g all-purpose flower with ⅔ teaspoon salt and 1½ teaspoons baking soda)
- 50 g (1¾ oz/⅓ cup) Dutch (unsweetened) cocoa powder
- 480 g (1 lb 1 oz/2 cups) caster (superfine) sugar
- 4 eggs, lightly beaten
- 2¾ tablespoons vegetable oil
- 100 ml (3½ fl oz/⅓ cup) milk

icing & decorations

- fondant (see page 207), coloured for farm animals of your choice
- one quantity buttercream (page 205), coloured green
- grass piping nozzle

Makes 12–16 cupcakes

Start by making the fondant farm animals using the photo above as your guide. Fondant is pretty much like playdough – only edible. You can roll the fondant into balls, and stick the balls together with a little water. You can also make little field flowers (or buy them from the baking aisle in the supermarket).

Preheat oven to 160°C (320°F).

Place the butter, chocolate and water in a double boiler over low heat and stir until melted. Sift the flours and cocoa into a large bowl. Stir in the sugar and make a well in the centre. Combine the eggs, oil and milk, then pour into the well in the dry ingredients and stir. Add the melted chocolate mixture and stir with a large spoon or spatula until completely combined.

Scoop the mixture into cupcake cases and bake for 20 minutes, or until a skewer poked into the middle comes out mostly clean – it's okay if it's a little sticky, but not wet.

Leave to cool completely.

Use a piping bag topped with a grass (fur) tip to apply the grass for the cupcakes. Pop the cupcakes in the refrigerator to harden for 30 minutes before positioning the fondant animals and flowers.

Store in an open cake box in a cool place (but not the refrigerator or they will become sticky) until ready to serve.

party favours

additional ideas
lolly bags with farm animal faces (page 48); playdough eggs with a plastic hen (page 73); matchbox treasure filled with colourful gems or lollies (page 169)

farm favour bags

• pink and black felt
• holepunch
• hot glue gun
• hessian (burlap) bags
• needle and twine

Make a simple felt pig by cutting a pink felt circle for the face, two triangles for the ears and an oval for the snout. Punch out two black felt circles for eyes. Use tiny bits of black felt for the nostrils, or draw them onto the nose using black marker pen. Make a tail by cutting some pink felt into a spiral (cut a round shape first, then begin cutting from its outside and work your way towards the middle of the circle along its curve). Use hot glue to assemble the piggy, then stick the face and tail onto the bag. Finish by using a needle to thread some twine through the top of the bag and tying it in a bow.

tic-tac-toe

• black, red and yellow paint
• small black stones (eight per bag)
• little hessian (burlap) bags
• black marker pen
• string

Paint bees and ladybirds onto small, flat black stones to use to play tic-tac-toe. Use the marker pen to draw lines on the hessian bags and pop eight stones into each one. Loosely tie the bags closed with string.

baa baa felt balls

• felt
• toy eyes (from craft shops) or embroidery thread
• 2.5 cm (1 in) felt balls
• hot glue gun

Cut sheep faces from felt (use the image above as a guide – you can also create mini pigs, cows and other farm animals) and sew little eyes on. Alternatively, use embroidery thread to make eyes if making these for very young children. Use hot glue to stick the faces to felt balls.

dinosaurs

they romp, they roar!

It's a verifiable fact that everyone loves dinosaurs. They are the heroes in this party – you'll need plenty of them and they'll need party hats and lots of fun things to do.

decorations

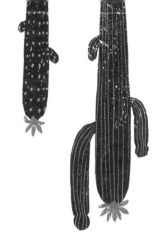

Decorate the party table with dinosaurs galore and a little greenery for the herbivores.

tassel and balloon garland

- tissue paper tassels (from party supply shops)
- balloons
- brightly coloured string
- small wooden pegs

Attach tassels and balloons to string with pegs to make this simple but fun garland.

dinosaur party hats

- card in various colours
- hot glue gun or stapler
- string
- small felt balls or pompoms

Make party hats for your little guests, but don't forget the dinos!

To create your cone shape, take coloured card and draw a circle with a radius of 20 cm (8 in) – use a compass to get an even shape. Cut out the circle and then cut a small triangle out of the circle (as if you're taking a sliver of pie). This will leave you with a gap in your circle, but means the ends of your cone will join up nicely.

Next, take the two ends created by the triangle cut-out and bring them together, folding one end under the other to create your cone. You can adjust the size and shape of your party hat by folding more of the card underneath the other end. When you are happy with the shape of the hat, hold your cone in place using the hot glue gun (or staple it together in a couple of places). Cut two pieces of string and either glue or staple one end of the string to two sides of the cone. The string pieces should be long enough so they can be tied together in a bow under each child's chin.

Now, let's jazz up your dinosaur party hat! Cut out three small triangles from different coloured cards (these will be the dinosaur spikes), fold the bottom edge of each triangle under the side of the cone and glue in place. Lastly, add a pompom to the top of your hat with hot glue. You could cut off the tip of the hat to make it easier to fix the pompom in place.

For your miniature dino friends, repeat the same steps to create the cones, but draw circles with a radius of 4–5 cm (1½–2 in). Forget about the spikes for these smaller party hats, but the pompoms are worth keeping. Dinosaurs like pompoms, in case you didn't know.

pterosaur nest

- foam balls (from craft stores)
- paint
- straw and fresh or artificial greenery

Paint the foam balls in colours of your choice. You can splash some of the paint on to create a dinosaur egg effect. Shape a nest out of straw, add your pterosaur eggs and then surround the nest with a little vegetation.

activities

dinosaur action

. . . .

- dinner plate
- card in two different colours
- black marker pen
- split pin
- minute egg timer

Place a dinner plate on one of the coloured cards, trace around it and cut out the circle. Using the marker pen, divide your circle into six wedges. Label each wedge with a type of dinosaur: stegosaurus, triceratops, pterodactyl, brontosaurus, velociraptor, tyrannosaurus rex. You can also add little dinosaur pictures – search online for free printables. Cut out an arrow shape from the other coloured card and attach it to the middle of the game board with a split pin. Check that it can spin easily. You're ready to play.

Explain the rules below to the children and talk about the different dinosaurs and what they might be like. For instance:

- stegosaurus (peaceful herbivore that walks on four legs and loves to eat leaves)
- triceratops (herbivore with a feisty nature, prone to quarrelling)
- pterodactyl (flying predator)
- brontosaurus (huge, slow-moving herbivore with a very long neck)
- velociraptor (small, speedy egg stealer)
- tyrannosaurus rex (basically, this is the bad dude, wants to eat everyone all the time)

Each child has a turn spinning the arrow. Before spinning, turn the egg timer over to start counting. It's game on. For one minute, all the children have to act like the dinosaur that the spinner lands on — *except* if the spinner lands on tyrannosaurus rex. If it lands on the tyrannosaurus rex, the adult gets one minute in which to eat as many little dinosaurs as they can catch.

hatchlings

. . . .

- balloons
- small plastic dinosaurs
- bowl large anough to hold all dinosaur eggs
- bowl of warm water
- plastic eye droppers

Give the balloons a good stretch before squeezing the dinosaurs through the opening. Hold the balloons under a tap and fill with water so that they are about twice the size of the dinosaur inside. Close the balloons by tying a knot and place in the freezer. When they are completely frozen you can cut the knot off the end and peel off the balloon.

When it's time to hatch the dinosaurs, you'll need an empty bowl to put all the eggs in and a bowl of warm water for the kids to fill their eye droppers and drop water on the eggs to help their dinosaurs break free from their icy shells!

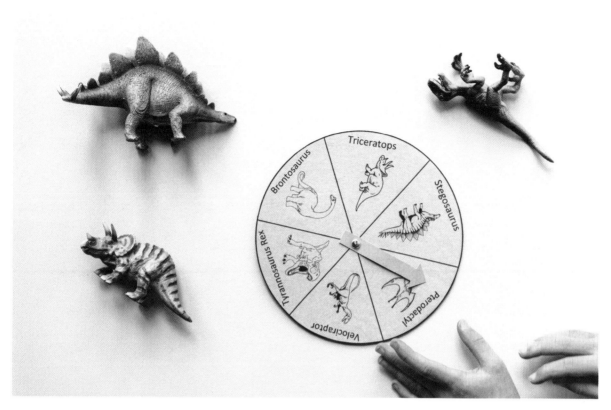

activities

dinosaur terrarium

- wide-mouthed jars (one per child)
- scoria (from garden supply stores)
- sand
- cuttings from succulent plants such as jade, pig face or little air plants
- small pebbles, stones, coloured gems
- plastic dinosaurs

The plants I've suggested are really hard to kill … it's all about the dinosaurs anyway. Get the kids to pour some scoria on the bottom of their jar, then let them sprinkle on some sand. Next, they'll need to add another layer of scoria and shake gently so that it settles. You might need to help with the following bit: poke a plant into the top layer – not too deep; it just needs to be stable. Have a selection of rocks, pebbles, coloured gems and a dinosaur for each child available. Let the kids decorate their terrariums, then label the jars with the kids' names and pop them into their favour boxes to take home later.

digging for bones

- 2 cups plain (all-purpose) flour
- 320 g (11½ oz/1 cup) salt
- 250 ml (8½ fl oz/1 cup) water
- picture of bones for inspiration
- sand pit or large tub filled with sand
- garden trowels, sifters and brushes for excavation work
- large cardboard box or sheet

Preheat your oven to 120°C (250°F).

Mix the flour, salt and water until combined, turn out on the kitchen bench and knead until nice and smooth like playdough.

Shape the dinosaur bones – use a picture of real bones to get ideas. Make little bones, big bones and long bones. Bones, bones, bones. When finished, bake in the oven for around three hours.

Bury your bones in a sand pit or large tub and arm the children with tools to dig them out. Have a box or sheet on the ground for the children to lay out the bones and let them guess at the species and body part.

food

carnivore food

- meatballs from the local butcher or delicatessen
- toothpicks

It's the name that's important for this one. Strictly for the carnivores.

herbivore fruit shapes

- rockmelon, watermelon and honeydew
- dinosaur-shaped cookie cutters

These fresh fruits come to life when cut into fun shapes with dinosaur cookie cutters.

pterosaur nests

- 1 packet fried noodles
- 250 g (9 oz) dark chocolate, melted
- sugared almonds or Mentos

Makes 10–12

Tip the noodles into a big bowl, pour over the chocolate and mix well. Place small clusters of the mix onto baking paper (parchment) to make mini nests. Rest the sugared almond eggs on the nests while the chocolate is still slightly gooey. Place in the refrigerator to set.

footprint cookies

- basic cookie dough (page 215)
- plastic dinosaur
- small amount of extra flour

Makes 20–24

Line a baking tray with baking paper (parchment).

Make a batch of basic cookie dough. After the initial chilling, roll the dough into balls. Dip your friendly dinosaur's foot in the flour and then stamp a footprint on the cookies. Lay them out on the baking tray and put in the freezer for 30 minutes to chill.

Preheat the oven to 180°C (350°F).

When the cookie dough is chilled, bake for 18–20 minutes, until slightly golden.

lava flow & swamp water

- card in black and red
- glue
- double-sided sticky tape
- red and green cordial (syrup)
- soda water or lemonade (lemon-lime soda)
- leaves

Cut black card into a volcano shape (use the image on the top right as a guide). Next, cut lava from red card, glue it onto the black card and tape the volcano to a bottle. Fill with soda water and red 'lava' cordial.

For the swamp water, wind leaves around a bottle (you can hold them in place with a bit of sticky tape) and fill it with soda water and green cordial.

cake

drippy dinosaur cake

Make the easy chocolate cake on page 213. Remember to cut off the top of the cake to create a flat surface.

- half quantity of chocolate Swiss meringue buttercream (page 206)

chocolate icing
- 290 g (10 oz) dark chocolate
- 50 g (1¾ oz) butter, unsalted
- 1 tablespoon vegetable oil

decorations
- 250 g (9 oz) Maltesers (or Whoppers), smashed
- plastic dinosaurs
- dinosaur party hats (see page 64; optional)

Serves 16

This cake uses two types of icing to create the melting landscape effect.

Make a half quantity of chocolate Swiss meringue buttercream and do a crumb coat (page 204). Chill the cake in the refrigerator for at least 30 minutes, then do a second coat of buttercream and chill again.

While the coated cake is chilling make the chocolate icing. Melt everything together over a double boiler. Pour the warm icing onto the top of the cake. Make it nice and drippy – channel your inner lava flow. Chill again, then top with the smashed Maltesers (you could add a couple of whole ones too). Arrange dinosaurs and accessories. Roar.

party favours

additional ideas

stretchy toy dinosaurs;
dinosaur eggs (sugared
almonds, Kool Mints);
matchbox treasure filled
with coloured gems
(page 169)

dinosaur party boxes

- plain, round cardboard boxes with lids
- white and pale green paint

I suggest using boxes for these favours because the children will need to put their terrarium somewhere safe. Simply splatter the boxes with white and pale green paint. Dinosaur eggs!

colourful dinosaur eggs

- playdough in six different colours
- small airtight plastic containers
- twine
- small plastic dinosaurs

Roll playdough into colourful balls, pop them in the plastic containers and use some twine to tie a dinosaur friend to the top.

dinosaur socks

- pair of long socks for each child
- felt in one or two colours
- fixing pins
- sewing machine or overlocker

You'll need five felt spikes for each sock. Trace a spike from the template on page 219, or create your own. Cut out the spikes. Turn a sock inside out and cut a straight line with sharp scissors from just below the top elastic band to around 4 cm (1½ in) above the heel.

Place the spikes inside the sock with their edges lining up with the cut edge of the sock. Pin in place. Machine-sew along the seam. Repeat with the other sock.

Now turn your socks the right way around to reveal the spikes!

sprites, fairies & pixies

fern fronds & fairy friends

Create a magical world for your little fairy-lover with this sweet party.

decorations

Fairies, pixies and sprites are nature lovers: they like leafy fern fronds to hide behind and toadstool houses to live in. They have ladybirds as pets and ride squirrels for transport. They're extremely fond of pretty flowers, bird song and English breakfast tea and they much prefer the company of children to adults. Decorate accordingly.

get leafy

- fresh pine needles, fern fronds or palm leaves

Decorate your home and the party table with greenery. If you don't have access to anything leafy, ask your neighbours, or visit your local florist and see if they can get some in for you. Or make your own leaves from green card in various shades.

flowery headbands

- fresh cottage flowers
- leafy greenery
- twine

Make headbands for the children from gathered leaves and flowers: eucalyptus, cottage flowers, whatever you can find. Depending on the plant material, you may need twine to bind the leaves together. Display the headbands for the children to choose from and wear when they arrive.

fairy garden

- doll's house furniture, fairy-sized tables and chairs
- card cut into window and door shapes
- paper
- ribbon or string
- coloured pen

Create a magical fairy world in your garden with miniature doors, windows, itty-bitty tables and chairs, toadstools, tiny houses and more. Don't worry if you don't have a garden; attach some little dollhouse doors and windows to a wall inside so the children can imagine who lives there. Write secret fairy messages on paper, roll into scrolls, tie with ribbon or string and leave them for the kids to find.

activities

popsicle stick fairies

- paper doilies
- popsicle sticks
- origami paper
- coloured matchsticks (from craft or office supplies stores)
- glue sticks
- coloured pencils

Have the components of this activity ready to go.

Cut paper doilies into quarters to use as wings, cut circles for fairy faces, glue popsicle sticks into triangles and cut triangles of pretty origami paper for dresses. Supply coloured matchsticks for legs and pencils to draw the faces.

Let the children pick and choose from the materials to make their fairy.

magic fairy bells

- assortment of different coloured yarn
- sticks
- wooden beads
- jingly bells

Fairies love the tinkling sound of little bells.

Create an example bell before the party to give the children inspiration (use the image opposite as a guide).

On the day, have your materials ready to go. Show the children how to wrap the yarn around a stick, then help them add beads and jingly bells to make their own magic fairy bells.

When the bells are finished, tie string to both ends of the stick so it can be suspended.

decorate fairy wings

- card
- tape
- string
- pens
- glue sticks
- glitter
- paper doilies
- sticker gems
- felt circles

Prepare the fairy wings before the party.

Cut a butterfly shape from card in a colour of your choice using the top left photo as a guide (you can either cut the wings in one piece or assemble them from multiple pieces of card – you could even have different colours for the body and wings). Attach string loops on either side of the wings with tape to create arm holes for the children.

Let the kids decorate their wings with pens, glitter, paper doilies and more.

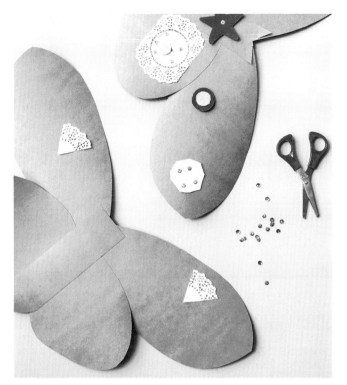

additional ideas
musical toadstools
(page 118); make a
terrarium (page 116);
decorate a
magic wand

food

flower sandwiches

- thin-sliced bread
- flower cookie cutter
- fillings of your choice

Use a flower cutter to make these peek-a-boo sandwiches. Do a few variations; for example, cream cheese and sprinkles, and cheese and ham.

fruit wands

- kebab sticks
- assorted fruit, cut into bite-sized pieces
- watermelon
- star cookie cutter

Thread fruit pieces onto kebab sticks (remember to cut the pointy ends off) and finish with a watermelon chunk cut into the shape of a star on top.

tasty toadstools

- 150 g (5½ oz) white chocolate, melted
- raspberry food flavouring
- 300 g (10½ oz/2 cups) strawberries, whole
- white sprinkles
- marshmallows

Makes 15–20

Use a little raspberry flavouring to colour the white chocolate pale pink. Cut the strawberry tops off at the fruit's widest point to create a flat suface and submerge the berries in the melted chocolate. Scatter with white sprinkles while still wet and attach them upside down to the marshmallow bases (use extra white chocolate if needed to make the toadstools stick).

jam flowers

- 2 sheets shortcrust pastry
- flower cookie cutter
- icing (confectioners') sugar, for dusting
- jam

Makes 25–30

Preheat the oven to 200°C (400°F) and grease a baking tray.

Cut flower shapes from shortcrust pastry and place onto the baking tray. Bake for approximately 8 minutes, until golden. Let the flowers cool before removing from tray. When cool, sift icing sugar over them to coat the petals, then spoon the jam filling into the centre of the flowers.

pink drink

- pink lemonade (pink sparkling soda)
- fresh raspberries
- small bunch of thyme sprigs

Pour the lemonade into individual glasses and pop in a couple of fresh raspberries and a sprig of thyme.

cake

chocolate sponge cake with forest berries

....

Make the two chocolate sponge cakes on page 212.

filling

• 200 ml (7 fl oz) cream, for whipping

• raspberries or strawberries, quartered or sliced

• raspberry jam

garnish

• raspberries or strawberries with the tops left on

Serves 8–10

When you are ready to decorate the chocolate sponge, whip some cream for the filling. To make the whipped cream, use an electric mixer on high speed to whisk the cream until stiff peaks form.

Spread whipped cream onto the bottom sponge with a spatula. Top with the raspberries or strawberries. Heat the jam a little to make it runny, then drizzle it over the cream and fruit.

Place the other layer of sponge onto the cream and fruit. Pile strawberries or raspberries on top. You could also place small fresh, edible flower buds (see page 208) such as violets or orange blossom on the fruit.

party favours

additional ideas
pixie dust (fill miniature jars with glitter); rainbow dancing ribbon (page 20); felt acorns (page 125)

fairy favour bag

- paper party bags
- white paper doilies
- glue
- guineafowl feathers
- small wooden pegs
- sticker paper

Create pretty favour bags by gluing doilies cut to size onto simple paper bags, then attach the feathers with wooden pegs. Print the words 'thank you' on the sticker paper and adhere to the bags.

felt headband

- felt in two contrasting colours
- a thin plastic headband
- hot glue gun

Cut out two feather shapes from felt using the image opposite as a guide: one large (32 cm/12½ in) and one small (15 cm/6 in). Sew together using running stitch (there are excellent tutorials on embroidery stitches online if you need to brush up on your needlework knowledge). Use hot glue to stick the feathers onto the headband.

wooden peg fairies

- wooden peg dolls (from craft stores)
- pencil and acrylic paints
- paint brushes and toothpick
- clear matt varnish paint
- felt
- hot glue gun
- craft matchsticks or tiny twigs

You might need to lightly sand the doll before you start, but only if it feels a little rough.

Draw the face outline and details on the doll with a pencil. Hold the doll by the body and paint the head. Use a toothpick to dot on the eyes. Use a long, thin brush for the mouth. When the head is dry it's time to paint the body. Hold the doll by the head and paint on any pattern you like. When dry, finish with a coat of clear matt varnish (it will prevent chips and general grubbiness). Cut wings from the felt and use hot glue to affix them. Last, hot glue antenna to your doll – you can use skinny twigs or coloured craft matchsticks.

pirates & plunder

dust off your eye-patch & polish your wooden leg

Who doesn't want to be a pirate?
Not only do they have cool hook
hands and eye-patches, but they
get to have a pet parrot on their
shoulder, and when they are not
making people walk the plank they
are searching for gold. Yikes!
I want in on this caper.

decorations

Search for bounty in your shed (or your neighbour's) and dig out some old rope, bottles and wooden crates. Complement with plastic fish, shells, driftwood ... and treasure!

lost cargo

- old wooden crates or cardboard boxes
- fishing net or bird netting

Old wooden crates are easily transformed into smuggled goods. If you don't have crates, use cardboard boxes. Throw some netting on top – I used bird netting that I had handy, but you can get faux fishing net from party supply stores.

rope bottle

- double-sided sticky tape
- old rope
- old bottle

Attach the double-sided tape to the base of the bottle to about halfway up, then wrap some rustic-looking rope around it.

activities

pirate photo booth

- netting and/or treasure map for backdrop
- hooks, temporary tattoos, eye-patches, pirate hats

Arrange some netting or a large treasure map as a backdrop. Then set up a table with hooks, tattoos, eye-patches, pirate hats and other pirate paraphernalia for children to choose from. Stuffed parrots are another great accessory.

The photos make for a fantastic party memory. You could have them printed and send them to your little guests and their parents as a thank-you note.

walk the plank

- balance beam or plank
- blue sheet of tarpaulin
- plastic sharks and fish

Place the plank over the tarpaulin and surround it with sea critters.

Get the little pirates to make their way across the plank one by one. You can add some extra challenges for older children. Ask them to walk the plank backwards, or blindfolded or – for a hot summer's day – shoot them with water pistols while they are crossing the plank.

hook ye a pretzel

- pretzels
- large serving bowl
- pirate hooks

Pour the pretzels into a large bowl and pass around the pirate hooks. You catch 'em, you crunch 'em!

activities

treasure hunt

- white paper, black marker pen and matches for the map
- box to hold the treasure
- the bounty: lots of chocolate gold coins, Ferrero Rocher chocolates (take off brown cases so they look like gold balls), strings of pearls, rubies, and other trinkets if you have them to hand
- kiddie-friendly trowels or spades to dig up the treasure
- cunning series of clues

First things first. Where be the treasure? If you have a spot outside where you can bury a box that's perfect – but wherever you hide the treasure you'll need some landmarks on your map to help the pirates find their way. Mark out a starting point on your map and a first clue – the idea being they get to the first landmark and solve the first clue to lead them to the second landmark and second clue and so forth. Mix up the type of clues: word puzzles, jigsaw puzzles etc.

To make your map and clues look authentically piratey, draw with black ink on white paper and then carefully hold a match to the edges. (STOP: you might want to run a copy of your map off on the photocopier before you proceed with the matches.) Don't go getting all pyro – you just want to singe the edges. If you hold the flame under the paper so it's *nearly* touching you'll get a nice aged effect. Maybe burn just a tiny little hole here and there. Not too much now. (You can also get the aged effect using tea, but personally I prefer the match method.)

For a large group of kids, divide your pirates into teams and away they go.

additional ideas

attach pirate hooks to a board and have the kids throw quoits onto the hooks for a game of pirate hook toss; shark piñata; decorate pirate hats made from card

food

croissant crabs

- edible eyes (from cake supply stores or supermarkets)
- toothpicks
- writing icing
- croissants
- filling for the croissants (optional)

Attach edible eyes to toothpicks using writing icing. Cut and fill the croissants however you like. Add the eyes before serving.

starfish sandwiches

- thin-sliced bread
- star cookie cutter
- fillings of your choice

Make up the sandwiches with the cookie cutter, then stack 'em high and watch 'em fly.

oyster surprise

- apricot yoghurt balls
- mini foil cupcake cases
- writing icing
- edible eyes (from cake supply stores or supermarkets)

Put the apricot yoghurt balls in mini cupcake cases and fold over the foil. Use writing icing to glue the eyes on top.

shark fin jelly

- grey fondant (see page 207)
- 8 popsicle sticks
- 85 g (3 oz) blue jelly (Jell-O) crystals
- 8 small (150 ml/5 fl oz) glasses
- 250 ml (8½ fl oz/1 cup) cream, for whipping

Makes 8

Make two shark fins per glass from grey fondant. Sandwich a popsicle stick between the two fins by gently pressing them together.

Make up the jelly following the packet instructions, fill glasses to two-thirds full and allow to set. Whisk the cream using an electric mixer on high speed until soft peaks form. Top the jelly with whipped cream.

Poke the finned popsicle stick into the cream just before serving.

pirate punch

- small bottles or glasses
- striped straws
- twine
- double-sided sticky tape
- ginger ale

Bottles with pirate style! Wrap a bottle with the tape then wind around some sea-worthy twine. Tie straws (stripes please!) onto bottles with some more twine. Fill with ginger ale or – for the foolhardy – lemonade (lemon-lime soda) with a dash of blue food colouring.

cake

'Thar Be Treasure' cake

Use the method for the white cake recipe on page 210 – but use the quantities given here as you are only making four layers.

- 280 g (10 oz/2 cups) plain (all-purpose) flour
- 1 tablespoon bicarbonate of soda (baking soda)
- ¼ teaspoon salt
- 145 g (5 oz) unsalted butter, at room temperature
- 300 g (10½ oz/1⅓ cups) caster (superfine) sugar
- 3 egg whites, at room temperature
- 1 teaspoon clear imitation vanilla extract
- 240 ml (8 fl oz/1 cup) full-cream (whole) milk, at room temperature
- royal blue gel paste food colour
- sky blue gel paste food colour
- half quantity of Swiss meringue buttercream (page 206)
- chocolate gold coins
- 155 g (5½ oz/1 cup) blanched almonds or digestive biscuits, finely ground

seashells (optional)

- 80 g (2¾ oz) white chocolate, melted
- shell-shaped silicone mould

decorations (optional)

- small treasure chest
- little plastic sea creatures
- plastic palm tree

Serves 16

If you have a silicone shell mould, make some white chocolate shells for the 'beach' by pouring the melted white chocolate into the mould and letting your shells set in the refrigerator.

Preheat the oven to 160°C (320°F) and prepare four round 20 cm (8 in) cake tins.

Pour equal amounts of the batter into two bowls. Colour one bowl with the royal blue colouring and the other with sky blue. Go slowly – as soon as you reach a colour you are happy with, stop. The cakes will taste bitter if you add too much food colouring.

Divide the batter between the four cake tins. Bake the cakes as on page 210.

When the cakes are cool, use a round cookie cutter to cut the centre from the four cakes. Place a dark blue cake onto your cake stand and use a spatula to apply the buttercream. Next place a light blue cake and top with buttercream. Repeat, alternating dark and light until you reach the top. Give the whole cake a light crumb coat (page 204). Once the crumb coat has set, put the final layer of buttercream on.

Fill the hole with chocolate gold coins. If you have a mini treasure chest position it in the hole. Otherwise fill the hole to the top.

Make the sand by grinding blanched almonds (or biscuits) in a food processor and cover the cake, hiding the gold coin treasure inside it. (Use the palm of your hand to press the 'sand' onto the cake.) Decorate with chocolate shells, little plastic ocean critters and a plastic palm tree (optional).

party favours

treasure favour bag

- brown paper lunch bags
- chocolate gold coins
- small wooden pegs

Scan the treasure map you made for the treasure hunt (page 92) and print it directly onto brown paper lunch bags. You'll want to add some gold coins to these bags. You can never have enough gold. Close with a peg.

treasure boxes

- paper
- black marker pen
- craft matchboxes
- coloured gems (available from craft stores)

Cut out small paper shapes and draw on a skull and crossbones. Glue onto plain matchboxes. Fill them with tiny coloured gems.

felt fish

- orange felt
- blue sequins
- blue bugle beads
- small black beads for eyes
- blue embroidery thread
- fixing pins
- stuffing

Even pirates need a snuggly friend and this cute little fishy is just the ticket. You can use the template on page 221 or simply trace around a drinking glass to create two orange felt circles for the fish body. Cut two fin shapes and one tail.

Hand sew (or use a hot glue gun) the sequins onto the top of the fish in any pattern you like. Decorate the tail and fins with bugle beads or some fancy stitching. Add the eyes. Pin the tail and fins in place between the top and bottom of the fish body. Use blanket stitch to sew from one side of the tail, all the way around the whole fish to the other side of the tail (there are excellent tutorials on embroidery stitches online if you need to brush up on your needlework knowledge). Fill with stuffing and sew closed.

additional ideas

plastic shells and sea
critters; pirate tattoos;
marshmallow poppers
(page 181)

space

launch into some intergalactic fun

Before the party day, brush up on
your planetary knowledge and
be prepared to be asked the
tricky questions.

decorations

Are they out there? You can ponder the existence of alien life forms and debate the origins of the universe while you decorate for this cosmic party. (And listening to David Bowie is a must.)

recreating space

- metallic silver paint
- paint brush
- black sheet or large piece of black card
- silver star stickers (optional)
- paint in various colours
- foam balls in various sizes (from craft stores)
- invisible thread

It's not every day you get to recreate the universe, but here's your shot at it. Using a paint brush, flick the silver paint onto the black sheet or card to create distant stars for your backdrop. If you like, add bigger stars using silver star stickers like those you used to get when you did good work at primary (elementary) school.

Create some colourful planets by making swirls of paint on the backdrop card or by painting foam balls. You can then suspend your planets from the ceiling with the invisible thread.

space plates

- blue plastic plates
- white writing icing

I dabbed white writing icing on the plates to make tiny stars (see the image on page 109). If serving the flatbread rockets (page 108), work out where the rockets are going to sit and use the icing to add stars so that they are all ready to go.

rocket bottles

- small glass bottles
- card in various colours
- double-sided sticky tape

Cut wings and windows from coloured card and stick them onto little glass bottles to turn them into rockets (see the image on page 109 for inspiration).

activities

build a rocket

- toilet paper rolls
- white paper
- glue
- card in three colours
- red tissue paper
- sticky tape
- black marker pen

Create a couple of rockets beforehand and have them on display to inspire the kids.

Wrap the paper roll in white paper and glue in place. Create the rocket top – cut an 8 cm (3¼ in) diameter semi-circle from card, bring the straight sides together and fold them over each other to form a cone shape, then fix in place with glue or tape. Make two triangle wings out of card, then cut two large circles and two slightly smaller circles in a different colour for the windows. Cut thin strips of red tissue paper for the rocket stream.

To assemble, put glue around the top of the paper roll, then affix the cone. Glue the windows in place. Fold the triangles over at the base and glue the base to the paper roll so the wings stand out from the rocket body. Use tape to attach the red tissue paper jet stream on the inside of the rocket. Using a pen, draw on a friendly face peeking out of a window.

Prepare all rocket elements in advance and let the little astronauts build their own shuttles.

create a moonscape

- moon sand – 8 cups plain (all-purpose) flour to 1 cup vegetable oil
- large shallow bucket or basin
- rocks in various sizes
- plastic aliens, rockets and other space paraphernalia

Make the moon sand by mixing the flour and oil in a bowl. Pour it into a large bucket or basin. Pile some rocks, aliens and space toys into the middle of the container. Add children.

activities

additional ideas

whack an alien piñata; outer
space obstacle course;
make green alien slime
(there are heaps of
recipes online)

straw rockets

· sugar sachets
· coloured paper
· straws
· glue

Pick up some little sugar stick sachets from your local café to make these super cool rockets. Fold down the corners on one end to make a point and glue them into place. Tear off the other end to create an opening (and dispense the sugar into your coffee). Finally, glue on colourful paper triangles and circles as wings and windows. Pop a straw into the open end of your rocket, blow and shoot it into outer space.

Depending on the age of your partygoers, you can prep some of the stages above (for example, have pre-cut windows and wings ready to go) or let them do the whole thing themselves.

UFO toss

· 3 buckets or hula hoops
· 5 frisbees
· card
· marker pen

Position the buckets or hoops to represent planets and attribute points to them. For example, 10 points for Mars because it's closest to Earth, 20 for Saturn and 30 for Pluto.

Each child gets a turn to toss the five frisbee UFOs into the planets. Whoever gets the most points wins – keep track by drawing up a table on card with a column for each child.

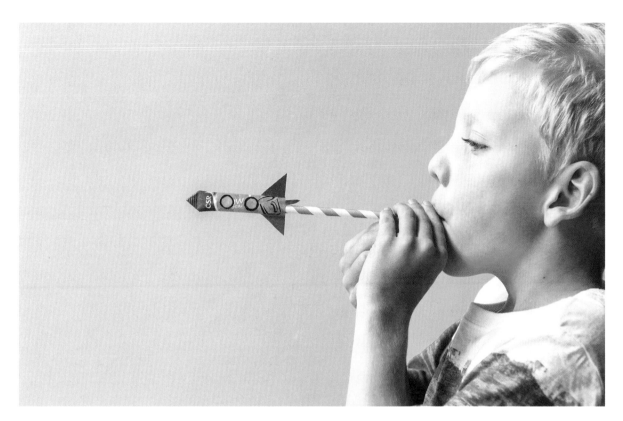

food

UFO buns

- fondant (see page 207)
- round bread rolls
- writing icing
- toothpicks or mini forks
- fillings of your choice

Make fondant circles for the UFO windows. When you are ready to assemble, cut bread rolls in half. Use writing icing on the back of the fondant circles to stick them to the top of the bread roll. Poke three toothpicks or mini forks into the base of each bread roll so the UFO sits up on legs. Now fill your buns and assemble.

rocket flatbread

- flatbread or pita
- hummus
- cucumber circles
- carrot strips or red capsicum (pepper)

Spread a flatbread with hummus, then fold and wrap the flatbread into a triangle to make the rocket nose. Take the bottom corners and fold them back on themselves so that they poke out to make the wings – you can cut to shape if you're not happy with the wings' angle. Add cucumber windows and cut carrot or red capsicum into strips to make the jet stream. Position on a space plate (page 102) and they're ready for take-off.

alien fruit platter

- edible eyes (from cake supply stores or supermarkets)
- toothpicks
- writing icing
- strawberries, rockmelon, watermelon, cut into small pieces

Stick edible eyes to toothpicks using writing icing. Poke your eyeball sticks into pieces of fruit.

it-comes-from-outer-space jelly cups

- 85 g (3 oz) green jelly (Jell-O) crystals
- 250 ml (8½ fl oz) cream, for whipping
- edible eyes (from cake supply stores or supermarkets)
- marshmallows
- green writing icing
- green bendy straws
- 8 small (150 ml/5 fl oz) glasses

Makes 8

Make up the jelly following the packet instructions and leave to set. Whisk the cream, using an electric mixer on high speed, until soft peaks form.

Stick the edible eyes onto the marshmallows with writing icing. Allow to set.

Layer jelly and cream in the glasses, finishing with a layer of green jelly. It's best to spoon set jelly into the cups rather than setting the jelly in the cups – otherwise it will look too neat (and be fiddly). Impale the marshmallow eyes onto the bendy end of the straws, then poke the straws into the jelly cups.

rocket fuel

- rocket bottles (page 102)

Fill with your choice of fuel.

cake

moon cake

- 600 ml (20½ fl oz/2¼ cups) cream, for whipping
- 55 g (2 oz/¼ cup) caster (superfine) sugar
- 1 teaspoon vanilla extract
- 500 g (1 lb 2 oz) chocolate ripple biscuits (any packaged chocolate cookie will do)
- white Swiss meringue buttercream (page 206)

decoration

- coloured card for the rocket
- glue and sticky tape
- kebab stick
- moon rocks (edible chocolate rocks, optional)

Serves 16

To make the whipped cream, use an electric mixer on high speed to whisk the cream until soft peaks form. Stir the sugar and vanilla through the whipped cream.

Select a bowl in the shape and size you want the cake to be. Line the bowl with plastic wrap, making sure you leave a long flap on each side – you will use this later to wrap the bottom of the cake. Now line the bowl with biscuits, then use a spatula to spread a thick layer of the whipped cream on top, making sure all the biscuits are completely covered in cream. Do another layer of biscuits, then cream, and so on until you reach the top of the bowl, finishing with a layer of cream. It should be flat across the top of the bowl. Pull the plastic wrap up from the sides of the bowl and place over the cake. Weigh down the cake with a plate and place the whole thing in the refrigerator for 24 hours.

Make a rocket by cutting the rocket body, wings, windows and the jet stream from card and gluing them together (use the image as a guide). Fix onto a kebab stick with sticky tape.

Make a batch of Swiss meringue buttercream as white as possible (page 206).

Retrieve the cake from the refrigerator and carefully invert it onto a cake plate and remove the plastic wrap. Do a crumb coat (page 204) with the buttercream, before finishing with a thick top coat. Use a spoon to create craters in the buttercream – some big, some small. Keep the cake in the refrigerator until ready to serve. Add the rocket. You can serve the cake with some edible rocks for extra outer space decoration.

party favours

additional ideas
marshmallow poppers (page 181); bouncy balls with a space pattern; glow-in-the-dark stars

favour rocket

- coloured card
- red tissue paper
- paper cups, for body of rocket
- wrapping paper or aluminium foil
- glue and sticky tape

Cut rocket wings from coloured card. Create a cone for the top of the rocket slightly bigger than the cup (see page 104; adjust the diameter of your semi-circle based on the size of your cup). Cut tissue paper strips for the jet stream. Glue wrapping paper onto the outside of the paper cup or wrap in foil, then add little card cut-outs as windows. Attach the wings and tissue paper strips. Fill with goodies. Join the cone lid to the cup by attaching tape to the inside of the cup and the lid on one side only (it should be able to lift up on one side to access the goodies).

space dough

- 1 cup plain (all-purpose) flour
- ½ cup salt
- 2 tablespoons cream of tartar
- food colouring
- 1 tablespoon vegetable oil
- 1 cup boiling water
- glitter
- small airtight plastic tubs

Put the dry ingredients into a large bowl. In a separate bowl, stir the food colouring, oil and boiling water together. Pour the liquids into the dry ingredients and mix well. Knead in the glitter. Divide it among the airtight plastic tubs.

alien key ring

- fusion beads in various colours
- square bead pegboard
- metal key ring finding and key chains

Follow the picture to recreate these alien key rings. Choose two contrasting colours and black for the eyes. Follow the packet instructions for setting the beads. When cool, thread the key ring finding through a hole in one of the beads at the top of the aliens' heads.

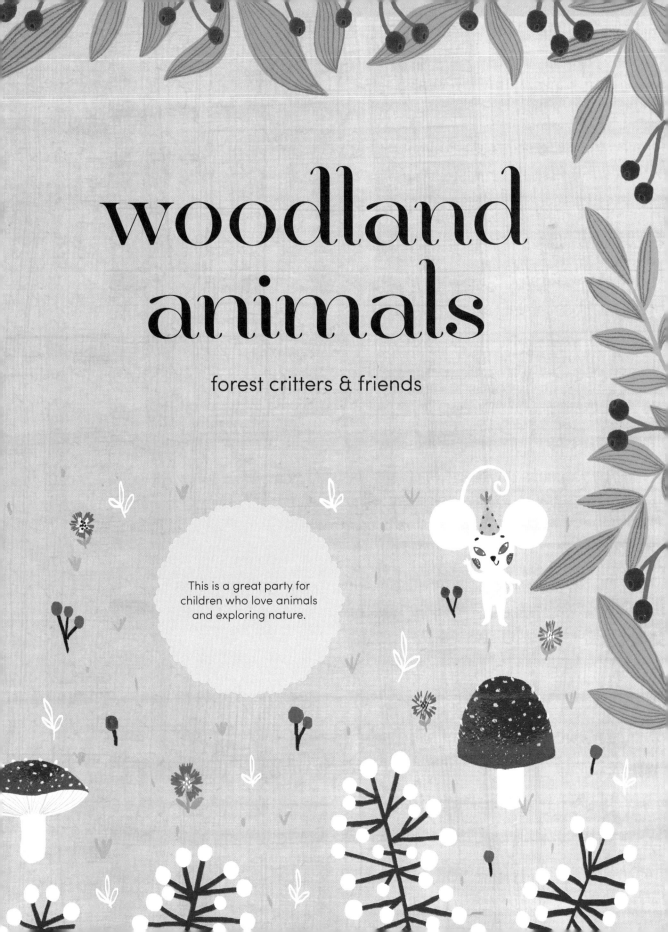

woodland animals

forest critters & friends

This is a great party for children who love animals and exploring nature.

decorations

Every season brings its own little bit of magic to the forest, whether it be the bright green of new leaves in spring, the reds and oranges of autumn leaves, or the many different nuts and cones scattered on the ground.

And while all kids love the traditional woodland animals — squirrels, foxes, bears, hedgehogs — you can put your own spin on it to suit where you live.

If you're having the party inside, you can decorate with leaf confetti, nature garlands, large branches and bunches of greenery suspended about the table or pinned to the wall.

woodland backdrop

- 2 large sheets of white card
- picture of deciduous trees to copy
- black marker pen
- fresh leaves (optional)
- poster putty or other adhesive

Draw tree trunks on the card, then cut them out and draw wood details on with black permanent marker. Add some fresh leaves if you like. A little forest of trees is nice. Fix them to the wall with adhesive.

circle leaf garland

- old children's books
- 4 cm (1½ in) holepunch (I used a flower shape for this garland)
- thread
- sewing machine

Punch out a nice variety of text and animals from the books and then pair them up.

Have a play with the tension on your sewing machine to make sure the stitches come out nice and even on the paper. Connect the paper circles into a garland by sewing a straight line through the middle of each paired circle. Make sure you leave around 1 cm (½ in) space between each circle – this will allow the garland to move freely and hang nicely.

When you're happy with the length, lay the garland out and carefully fold each circle in half so that you create three-dimensional circles.

Multiple strands of the garland look good together, or run a long single strand in horizontal loops on a wall.

leaf confetti

- leaves
- holepunch

It really is as simple as it sounds. Allow your leaves to dry out for a few days before punching out the confetti. Sprinkle on the cake table and surrounds.

activities

terrarium

- wide-mouthed jam jars
- small pebbles and stones
- sand
- scoria (from garden supplies stores)
- plant cuttings
  (succulents are a good option)
- small plastic figurines
  (squirrels, wombats, bears, etc.)

Get the kids to put some pebbles on the bottom of the jar, then sprinkle on some sand. They'll need to give it a gentle jiggle to let the sand sift through. Now the scoria, and a bit more sand. Time to do the jiggle dance again. You might need to help with the next bit: poke a hole on the surface layer and gently nestle the plant in place.

Finally, the children can choose some stones and plastic friends to artfully arrange in their terrarium.

forest friend headbands

- brown paper roll
- double-sided sticky tape
  or masking tape
- pairs of fresh leaves in a
  variety of colours and shapes
- black marker pen

These headbands can be prepared beforehand so that the kids just have to choose which ears (leaves) to stick on and draw a face. Cut the brown paper into strips and fit it to the size of your child's head. You can adjust on the day with sticky tape to fit each child's head.

On the day, set up a workstation with lots of leaves in different colours and shapes, marker pens and double-sided sticky tape. Have a few completed headbands on display so that the kids can see what the finished headbands will look like. Then help the children put some tape where they want the ears to go. Ask them to search for two matching leaves. What works for a rabbit, eagle, owl or a bear? Get them to draw some simple animal faces: just eyes and noses.

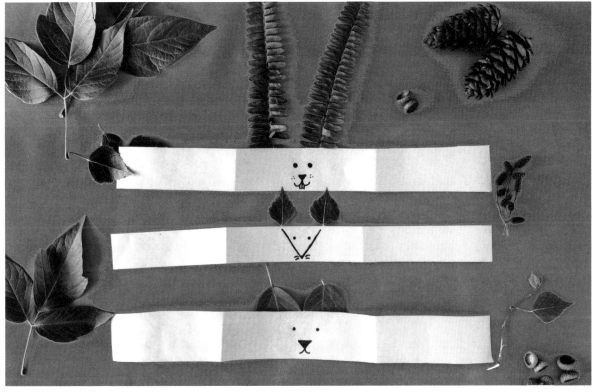

activities

nature scavenger hunt

- plain paper
- 2 clipboards
- string
- pencils
- 2 bags or baskets

Create an illustrated list of natural items appropriate for the season and location, and challenge the children to see how many they can find. Clipboards are great – they don't fly away in the wind and they're easier for the kids to manage than a loose piece of paper. (Also, one feels more 'serious' when sporting a clipboard.) Tie string around a pencil and attach it to the clipboard. Group the kids in two teams. Give them, say, five minutes to see how many they can find.

Each team should get a bag or basket to hold their found objects. To make it more fun, ask your nature hunters to measure objects against their body. For example, 'Find a leaf longer than your longest finger.'

Ask for sightings of wildlife rather than actual wildlife (or your pet guinea pigs may never forgive you).

Be sure to supplement your natural environment with some strategically placed added extras so that it's not too tricky.

musical toadstools

- red card
- white card
- double-sided sticky tape or glue

Make some large toadstools from red and white card for the children to sit on for a traditional game of musical toadstools.

To play the game you'll need one fewer toadstool than you have guests. Arrange the toadstools in a circle on the ground. The children must walk in a circle around the outside of the toadstools while music plays (an adult should be in charge of the music). When the music stops, the children race to sit on a toadstool. Whoever is left without a toadstool is out of the game (they can help 'judge' now). Take away one toadstool and start again. Each time the music stops someone is out and a toadstool is removed until you are left with two players and one toadstool. The winner is the child who sits on the very last toadstool.

For a twist on the game, ask the children to hop on one leg or skip instead of walking.

additional ideas
pin the tail on the deer (see page 42); nature obstacle course; hand-print bear (page 30)

food

bear buns

- white fondant (see page 207)
- pink gel paste food colour
- round bread rolls, cut in half horizontally
- black writing icing
- fillings of your choice

Prepare your bear's face by making little round white ears and an oval shape for the muzzle from white fondant. Next, colour some fondant pink to make two flat round cheeks. When you're ready to assemble, use writing icing to attach the fondant pieces to the top half of the bread rolls. Use the writing icing to draw eyes and a nose.

Fill your bears and serve.

cheesy toadstools with cherry tomato tops

- block of mild-tasting cheese
- cherry tomatoes
- toothpicks
- small amount of melted white chocolate or white writing icing

Cut cheese into smallish squares (1 cm/½ in), then use a vegetable peeler to take off the hard edges and sculpt them into circular toadstool trunks. Cut cherry tomatoes in half. Use a toothpick to dab spots onto the toadstool tops with melted white chocolate or white writing icing. Now stick the toadstools together with a toothpick – it's a good idea to remove the pointy end of the toothpick.

chocolate acorns

- wafers cut into circles
- Hershey's Kisses
- dark chocolate, melted

Line up your wafers and use a small circle cutter to punch out the acorn tops (I used a melon baller!). Unwrap your Kisses. Dab a bit of melted chocolate onto one side of the wafer and then stick the flat bit of the Hershey's Kiss on top. Add a little dollop of melted chocolate to the top of the acorn.

Fend off the squirrels and enjoy.

hedgehog cookies

Make a batch of the basic cookie dough as on page 215.

- 100 g (3½ oz) dark chocolate, melted
- sprinkles

Makes 20

After the first chilling of the dough, roll it into balls and pinch out a nose shape. Lay them out on a baking tray lined with baking paper (parchment) and put in the freezer for 30 minutes to chill. Preheat the oven to 180°C (350°F).

When chilled, bake for 18–20 minutes, until the noses are slightly golden.

When cool, dip your hedgehogs – bottom first – into melted chocolate. Submerge to a little over halfway. Rest on baking paper and decorate with sprinkles. When they are dry add the finishing touches using a skewer to dab a tiny bit of melted chocolate for two little eyes and a nose.

food

two types of lemonade infusions

watermelon & mint

- 100 g (3½ oz) watermelon, puréed
- 1 litre (34 fl oz) lemonade
  (lemon-lime soda)
- 8 mint leaves
- ice cubes

Mix the watermelon purée and lemonade together. Pour through a strainer into a pretty bottle and add mint. Add some ice cubes shortly before serving.

strawberry & basil

- 90 g (3 oz) strawberries, puréed
- 1 litre (34 fl oz) lemonade
  (lemon-lime soda)
- 3–4 basil leaves
- 3–4 quartered strawberries
- lemon zest
- ice cubes

Mix the strawberry purée with the lemonade. Add a few basil leaves, strawberries and a little lemon zest. Add some ice cubes shortly before serving.

cake

wholesome log cake

Make double the quantity of the easy chocolate cake recipe on page 213.

- ⅛ cup apricot jam
- chocolate Swiss meringue buttercream (page 206)
- Dutch (unsweetened) cocoa powder, for dusting

decoration

- felt acorns (page 125; optional)

Serves 24

Grease and line two 23 cm (9 in) round cake tins with baking paper (parchment). Bake the cakes at 160°C (320°F) for around 80–90 minutes. When cool, cut the cakes flat at the top.

When you are ready to ice, stack the cakes on top of each other, adding a little apricot jam between the layers. Make the chocolate Swiss meringue buttercream. Do a crumb coat (page 204).

When the crumb coat has set, pipe a spiral of icing onto the top of the cake, then smooth down with a spatula. Use a fork to create rings on the top of the log.

Now smear the icing onto the cake sides with a spatula. Don't make it too smooth. Use the back of a spoon to create vertical indentations up the side of the cake. Use a fork to gently rough up the grooves on the side of the cake.

Dust the top lightly with a tiny bit of cocoa powder. Go over the fork grooves again. The result should make the 'cut' top of the log a slightly different colour from the sides.

Finally, add some forest critters, acorns or other woodland-themed deco.

party favours

additional ideas

tic-tac-toe (page 61);
wooden spinning tops;
adapt baa baa felt balls
to a woodland animal
(page 61)

animal favour bag

- coloured card
- black marker pen
- hot glue gun
- hessian (burlap) bags
- twine

Cut out woodland animal shapes from coloured card (you can create little badgers, foxes, squirrels etc.), assemble the parts with glue and add faces with black pen. Hot glue the animals to hessian bags. Thread twine through the top of the bag. Ready.

make a bee

- sheoak seeds (or alder cones)
- yellow wool
- white felt
- white cotton thread
- small stick or twig

Sheoak seeds make nice, fat bees full of buzz. Alternatively, alder cones work just as well.

To make the bees, wind the wool around the cone and tie off in the middle.

For the wings cut an oval of roughly 1.5 cm x 4 cm (1 in x 2½ in) from white felt. Tie the wings in the middle using white cotton thread. Pull tight to create two gathered wings. Last of all, hot glue the wings onto the middle of the body.

Tie your bee to a small stick so it can fly. Buzz.

felt acorns

- acorn caps
- 1 cm (⅜ in) felt balls in various colours (available at craft stores)
- hot glue gun

Use hot glue to stick acorn caps to felt balls. Instant cuteness.

haunted house

ghosts, ghouls & great fun

Why wait for Halloween?
You can create this haunted
house party all year round.

decorations

Create a super spooky party with candelabras, wilted flowers, dead tree branches, spider webs, bats, decay and just a touch of doom and gloom. It's like being invited over to Miss Havisham's for lunch.

bat mobile

- black card
- sticky tape
- black cotton thread
- large stick

Use the template on page 216 to create your bats. I did a mix of mostly large and a few small bats. Use the tape to attach the thread to the bats and then hang them from a large stick at different lengths. Tie thread to two points of the stick and suspend it from the wall to make a bat mobile.

spider's web

- about 2 m (6½ ft) of cheesecloth
- double-sided sticky tape
- faux spider web (from party supply shops)

Cheesecloth makes a great spider's web. Buy a couple of metres of the stuff. Hang it across the width of your doorway and stick it in place. Now use scissors to cut different length strips. Tear and rub the cloth together between your palms. The rattier the better. For finer detail add some ready-made spider web.

spooky balloons

- clear latex balloons
- helium
- black tulle
- invisible thread

Get clear balloons filled with helium and cover them with black tulle. Tie the tulle at the ballons' base and attach them to invisible thread.

faded florals

- white flowers past their prime
- plastic spiders
- faux spider web (from party supply shops)

Vases of slightly past-their-prime white roses make a lovely centrepiece. Be sure to attach some small plastic spiders and, perhaps, a touch of spider web.

activities

ghost obstacle course

- old sheets
- black marker pen
- plastic snakes, lizards, spiders, rats
- several packets of faux spider web (from party supply shops)
- large sticks

Make ghost costumes out of old sheets by cutting out eye-holes and drawing around eyes and adding a mouth. Construct a spooky obstacle course using plastic beasties and lots of spider web. Make sure to include at least one spider web crawl tunnel – you can build it using sticks or poles.

spider egg piñata

- spider piñata (from party supply shops)
- round white sweets such as Kool Mints, Mentos or yoghurt-covered apricot balls
- lots of little plastic spiders

There's a creepy little surprise in this piñata. Instead of the standard sweets mix, fill it with spider eggs and baby spiders.

wrap the mummy

- one roll of toilet paper per child

Team the children up and instruct them to wrap one child in their group like a mummy. Award a prize for the most convincing mummy (get the children to help with the judging).

donut gobble

- donuts with holes
- string or cotton thread
- broomstick or large dead branch

Tie string around donuts and suspend them from a broomstick. First to scoff a whole donut without using their hands gets to shine in the light of eternal glory (or maybe wins a prize).

additional ideas
apple bobbing; pin
the spider on the web (see
page 42); eyeball
(page 132) and
spoon relay

food

bat party pies

- 1 sheet of shortcrust pastry
- bat-shaped cookie cutter
- frozen party pies (mini meat pies)

Preheat your oven following the packet instructions for the party pies.

Cut bat shapes from shortcrust pastry and place them on top of the frozen pies just before placing them in the oven. Bake according to the instructions.

Instant bat pies.

banana ghosts

- small and large chocolate chips
- bananas, peeled and cut in half

Press the chocolate chips into place on the bananas to make faces. Don't prepare too far ahead or the bananas will go icky.

These guys think they're spooky, but the truth is they're just so darn cute no one will be afraid of them.

chocolate spiders

- 250 g (9 oz) dark chocolate
- 200 g (7 oz) packet fried noodles
- edible eyes

Makes 10–12

Melt the chocolate and then mix it through the noodles in a big bowl. Spoon small clusters of the mix onto baking paper (parchment). Position the eyes while the chocolate is still slightly gooey. Allow to set.

eyeballs

- raspberry jam
- yoghurt balls
- edible eyes (from cake supply stores or supermarkets)

Apply a small dollop of raspberry jam to a yoghurt ball and stick an edible eye in place.

food

lime spiders

- milkshake glasses
- some strips of cheesecloth
- lime cordial (syrup)
- vanilla ice-cream
- lemonade (lemon-lime soda)

It's best to bring the glasses and all your ingredients to the table to serve.

Wrap a little cheesecloth 'spider web' around the glasses. Pour about 2 cm (1 in) of cordial into the glass, then jam a big scoop of ice cream into the glass and top up slowly with lemonade (lemon-lime soda).

Watch the green volcano.

cake

creepy chocolate cake

Make the easy chocolate cake on page 213.

- half quantity buttercream (page 205)
- blackberry jam
- blackberries, if in season

chocolate icing

- 290 g (10 oz) dark chocolate
- 50 g (1¾ oz) butter, unsalted
- 1 tablespoon vegetable oil

decoration

- blackberry or raspberry bramble, or some thorny rose stems

Serves 16

Cut the top of the cake off to make it level and then cut the chocolate cake in half horizontally.

Use buttercream and blackberry jam to sandwich the layers (the blackberry jam should dribble out). Chill the cake for 30 minutes.

While it is chilling, make the chocolate icing by melting the chocolate and butter with the oil over a double boiler. When the cake is chilled, dribble the icing over the top of the cake. Chill again to set the icing.

Wrap the base of the cake in a long blackberry or raspberry bramble (wear gardening gloves, and please only use brambles that haven't been sprayed with nasties). You could place some blackberries here and there around the cake if they are in season.

party favours

additional ideas
gingerbread vampires;
finger-puppet monsters; a
matchbox with a label saying
'Henry's Home' – inside is a
'pet' plastic spider nestled on
some faux spider web

bat favour bags

- black party bags
- black and white card
- glue
- small wooden pegs

Cut bat wings from black card and bat teeth from white card. Attach the wings to the back of the party bags with glue. Fold the top of the bags down into a triangular shape and glue the teeth onto the end of the triangle. Use small wooden pegs to close the bags. They are great suspended from a stick on the wall until it is time to hand them out.

glow-in-the-dark broomsticks

- craft paper
- glow sticks
- string

Cut thin strips of brown craft paper and tie onto the bottom of a glow stick.

red-backed lollipop spider

- lollipops with red wrapping
- black pipe cleaners
- self-adhesive googly eyes
  (from craft shops)

Wind the black pipe cleaners around the lollipop stick to make spider legs, then stick the googly eyes onto the spider 'body'.

candy wands

- a variety of sweets
- kebab sticks

Thread soft jellies and other sweet treats onto the sticks. Sugar anyone?

garden high tea

special friends, pretty frocks & yummy cakes

I'm excited by tea parties, but especially garden tea parties. Along with the delicious cakes and decorative teaspoons there are flowers and you get to wear an awesome dress and put flowers in your hair and drink tea ... well, not real tea, but pretend tea – and it's all so grown-up and so cool!

decorations

You can go to town with the decorations for this party ... the more the better! Tissue paper pompoms, pretty tablecloths, all manner of garlands and heaps of fresh flowers make for easy decorations.

teapot vases

• teapots
• fresh flowers

It's not a tea party without teapots. Dress some up with bunches of fresh seasonal flowers.

table settings

• forks and spoons
• coloured napkins
• paper doilies
• twine

Time to break out Great Aunt Ethel's decorative teaspoons. Wrap forks and spoons in a napkin and a lacy paper doily, then tie off with twine (see the image on page 147).

A pretty fan makes a nice addition if the weather is warm.

activities

additional ideas

magic fairy bells (page 78);
nature scavenger hunt
(page 118); a child-friendly
version of croquet

colourful flower craft

- card in a variety of colours
- glue sticks

Prepare ahead of time by cutting card into various flower petal and stem shapes (use the image opposite as a guide or come up with your own designs). Make up a few flowers to give the children inspiration.

Set up a craft table and let your little guests create their personal flower bouquets.

floral fascinator

- brown paper
- selection of flowers, leaves and feathers
- tape in a dispenser

These flowery headbands are fun to make and are a pretty party souvenir to take home.

Trace around an upturned drinking glass onto brown paper and cut out. Cut two 30 x 4 cm (12 x 1½ in) lengths of paper and tape them to either side of the circle. Have the plain headbands, a selection of flowers and a tape dispenser ready to go at the party.

The children only have to choose the flowers to stick on. You'll need to help the children fasten the finished headbands in place by overlapping and adjusting the two strips of paper to fit the child's head and then stapling in place. It should slip on and off easily.

stack the teacups

- child's plastic tea set

Children's tea sets are almost indestructible, but in any case, this game is best played on soft grass or sitting upon some pretty cushions.

Each child has a turn at seeing how many cups they can stack before the pile topples.

pass the teapot

- pretty teapot
- sweets and chocolates

This is basically pass the parcel with a teapot.

Fill a teapot with sweets and chocolates. Let the children sit down in a circle and turn on some music. The children now pass the teapot around while the music is playing. Every time the music stops the child who is holding the teapot gets to choose a sweet from the pot and is out. The last child left in gets the rest of the sweets ... best not to put too many in there.

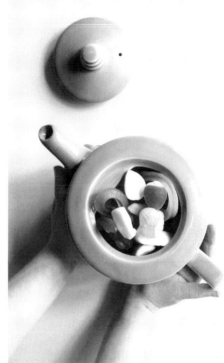

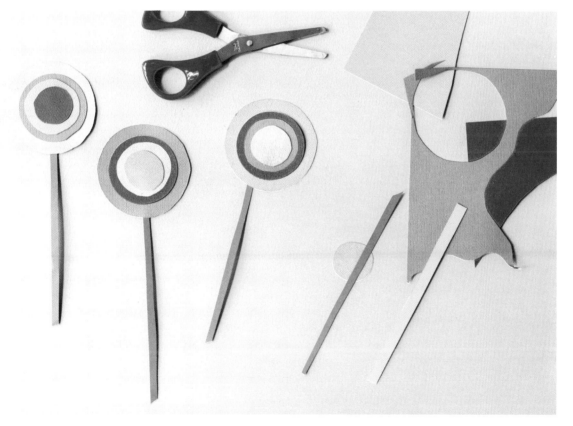

food

finger sandwiches

- thin-sliced bread
- cream cheese
- cucumber, thinly sliced
- violets or other edible flowers (page 208)

You'll want the tea party classic – cucumber sandwiches – but be sure to include a few other varieties. Dress them up with some pretty edible flowers such as violets.

berry delicious scones

- 450 g (1 lb/3 cups) self-raising flour (or 450 g all-purpose flour with 3 teaspoons salt and 6 teaspoons baking soda)
- 2 teaspoons baking powder
- 100 g (3½ oz) unsalted butter
- 250 ml (8½ fl oz/1 cup) milk, and a little extra for brushing the tops of the scones

to serve
- 200 ml (7 fl oz) cream, for whipping
- berry jam

Makes 18–22

Preheat your oven to 210°C (410°F) and line a tray with baking paper (parchment).

Lightly mix flour, baking powder and butter in a food processor until it is crumbly. Pour the mixture into a large mixing bowl and stir in the milk until just combined. Sprinkle some flour on your bench, turn out the dough and then lightly knead it until it just comes together. Roll the dough with a rolling pin until it is around 2½ cm (1 in) thick, then use a circle-shaped cookie cutter to press out the scones.

Place them close together in the centre of the baking tray and lightly brush with the extra milk. Bake for around 12 minutes, or until lightly golden on top.

You can make the scones ahead of time and simply top them with jam and whipped cream when you're ready to serve. To make the whipped cream, using an electric mixer on high speed, whisk the cream until soft peaks form.

marshmallow teacups

- marshmallows
- writing icing
- Arnott's Tic Toc biscuits (or any plain, round thin cookie)
- chocolate freckles (chocolate nonpareils)
- musk-flavoured Lifesavers, broken in half (mint Polos work, too)

Use writing icing to glue a marshmallow to a biscuit, then glue a freckle on top of the marshmallow. Finally, glue half a Lifesaver in place for the cup handle. Hold until it adheres.

food

teabag biscuits

Follow the recipe for basic cookie dough on page 215.

- 150 g (5 ½ oz) dark chocolate
- decorative coloured paper or card
- embroidery thread

Makes 30

Make the dough and when it is chilled, roll it out between two sheets of baking paper (parchment) until it is about 5 mm (¼ in) thick.

Cut out teabag-sized rectangles. Carefully cut off the top corners of your teabag biscuits. Use a straw to punch a hole in the top of the teabag (you'll use the hole later to thread the label on). Carefully lay out the biscuits on the baking tray and put back in the refrigerator for another 30 minutes to chill before baking as described on page 215.

When the biscuits are cool, melt the chocolate over a double boiler. Dip each biscuit into the melted chocolate about a third of the way up. Allow to dry on baking paper.

When the biscuits are ready, cut some little labels for the teabags from the decorative paper. Attach the labels through the hole in the biscuit with embroidery thread.

pink lemonade with floral ice cubes

- variety of small edible flowers, such as borage or violets (page 208)
- pink lemonade (pink sparkling soda)

To make the floral ice cubes, quarter fill an ice tray with water and freeze. When frozen, pop in little edible flowers face down and pour just enough water to almost cover the flowers. Freeze again. When frozen again, fill the ice tray up to the top. Add the floral ice cubes to pink lemonade for an extra special treat.

cake

mini red velvet cakes

Make the two red velvet cakes on page 214.

orange cream cheese icing

- 500 g (1 lb 2 oz) cream cheese, at room temperature
- 120 g (4½ oz) butter, unsalted, at room temperature
- 1 teaspoon vanilla extract
- 300 g (10½ oz/3 cups) icing (confectioners') sugar, sifted
- 1 teaspoon orange zest
- 1 teaspoon milk (if needed)

garnish

- fruit or fresh flowers (see page 208)

Makes 8

Once the cakes have cooled, use a long serrated knife to cut each cake in half horizontally. Use a circle-shaped cookie cutter to press out six rounds from each layer.

Beat the cream cheese and butter until just smooth. Stir through the vanilla, then add the sifted icing sugar a half cup at a time until combined. Stir through the zest. Taste test time. If the icing is a little too thick add a teaspoon of milk.

Pipe onto the mini cake layers and stack up the cakes. Garnish with fruit or fresh flowers.

party favours

additional ideas
felt acorns (page 125); felt ball bracelet (page 191); make a bee (page 125)

pretty fabric favour bags

- 2 x pieces of fabric 20 cm x 15 cm (8 in x 6 in)
- ribbon (for the closure)
- sewing machine

These bags are easily made with pretty fabric scraps. I've used two fabrics and covered the seam with rik rak, but you can just use one fabric for the whole bag. Sew the fabric pieces together, right sides facing. Leave open at the top and leave 3 cm (1¼ in) from the top open on one of the sides. Fold the top down by 3 cm (1¼ in) and press with an iron. Sew along the pressed-down seam, then turn the bag inside-out. Thread the ribbon through the seam.

felt teabags

- teabag
- white felt
- white cotton
- black embroidery thread
- felt in various colours for the labels
- white embroidery thread

Using the real teabag as your guide, cut out a teabag-sized rectangle from the white felt. Use running stitch to sew all the way around the edge of the teabag, folding down the corners (just like on your teabag) when you get to them. Use the black thread to sew on the name of the tea (mint, lemon, or simply 'tea') using cross stitch (there are excellent tutorials on embroidery stitches online if you need to brush up on your needlework knowledge). Add a felt picture if you like. Alternatively, just give the teabags a happy face. Add a long piece of white embroidery thread at the top of the teabag and attach the label. You can make the label from felt or use paper.

You could also use two pieces of felt sewn together for these bags. Stuff with some dried lavender for extra sweetness.

strawberry friend

- green, red and white felt
- saucer
- red, white and black embroidery thread
- small black beads
- fabric stuffing

Create green felt strawberry tops by cutting out multi-pronged star shapes. Put aside. Trace around a saucer on the red felt and cut out (do the same on white if you'd like to create white berries too). Cut the circle in half: each half will become a strawberry friend. Fold the semi-circle in half and sew the straight sides together with the red thread. Turn inside-out. Use the white embroidery thread to sew on some 'seeds' using French knot stitch. Add two little black bead eyes and a black embroidery mouth. Use running stitch to sew around the curved opening, then stuff before pulling the thread tight so that it gathers and closes up. Finally, sew or hot glue the strawberry tops on.

pancakes & pyjamas

pancakes, pyjamas & polka dots

The children will be so excited to come to a party in their pyjamas. I suggest making it early – any time after 8 am (it's not like anybody with small children sleeps in). And the best thing? Start early, finish early. It's all over by 11 am. Yeah!

decorations

We've gone dotty over this super cute party. Be sure to adorn the breakfast table with plenty of fresh fruit and pretty flowers. Fluffy slippers optional.

over-sized spotty garland

- card in various colours
- plate
- twine
- sticky tape

Use a plate to trace large circles on card and cut them out. Lay the circles out on the floor and arrange the colour sequences and spacing until you're happy. Get your twine and, leaving a tail of about 40 cm (15 in), tape the twine across the top third of your first circle, then your second circle, and so forth until you get to the end of your garland, leaving another tail at this end.

You can make multiple strands, or one super long strand to loop around at different angles.

confetti balloons

- clear latex balloons
- confetti
- helium (optional)
- string

Fill clear latex balloons with confetti by pouring it into the opening of the balloon with a funnel. You could fill the balloons with helium or simply blow them up the old-fashioned way – lung power. Attach to string so the kids can whack them around and watch the confetti bounce.

activities

additional ideas

popsicle stick fairies
(page 78); make a
bath bomb (page 186);
cardboard animal painting
(page 164)

Fruit Loop necklaces

- Fruit Loops
- large jar
- coloured twine, cut into
  necklace-lengths

Pour Fruit Loops into a pretty jar and supply the coloured twine for children to thread the loops to make their own necklace.

pancake relay

- plenty of pancakes
- 2 spoons or spatulas

Divide the kids into two teams. Each team gets a pancake on a spoon or spatula to relay. If you want to up the difficulty, get the kids to try and carry multiple pancakes at once!

paper donut craft

- craft card or thick paper
- pink and brown paper
- glitter, pompoms, felt balls,
  confetti, washi tape –
  you get the idea
- marker pens
- glue sticks

Cut paper donut shapes for the children. (A dinner plate and a glass are perfect for tracing around.) Now cut slightly smaller and squiggly donut shapes from the pink (strawberry) and brown (chocolate) paper to make icing that will fit onto the card.

Set up your donut crafting station with the pre-cut donuts, icing and little tubs with sprinkles, pompoms and other decorations to stick on top. Make sure you have at least three glue sticks on hand for the kids to share around.

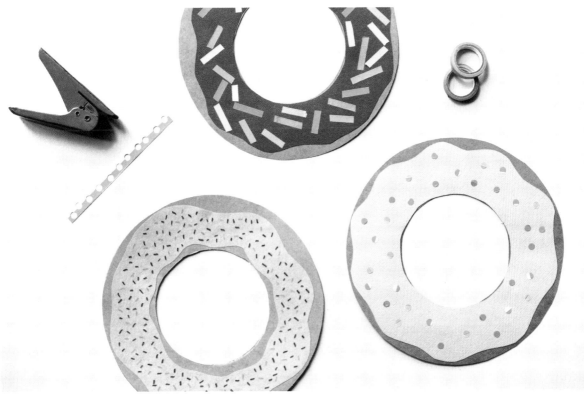

food

pancakes

- 300 g (10½ oz/2 cups)
  self-raising flour (or 300 g all-
  purpose flour with 2 teaspoons salt and
  4 teaspoons baking soda)
- 80 g (2¾ oz/⅓ cup) caster (superfine)
  sugar
- 340 ml (11½ fl oz/1⅓ cups)
  full-cream (whole) milk
- 2 eggs
- 1 teaspoon vanilla extract
- squeeze of lemon juice
- cooking spray

Makes 12–16

Sift flour into a large mixing bowl and add sugar. In a separate bowl, whisk together the wet ingredients. Fold the wet into the dry and mix until combined.

Spray a large frying pan with cooking spray and heat. Cook pancakes for around 2 minutes on each side – you want to see bubbles forming on the first side before you flip it. You can prepare these ahead of time and keep them snug wrapped in foil. When you're ready to serve, just warm through again under the foil in a preheated oven (160°C /320°F) for 5–7 minutes.

Serve with heaps of condiments, such as fresh fruit or whipped cream.

... and with blueberries

- punnet of blueberries

Same recipe as above but add a punnet of blueberries with the wet ingredients.

yoghurt & muesli with fruit

- plain yoghurt
- muesli
- fresh fruit or berries

Top small glasses filled with yoghurt with some crunchy muesli and fresh fruit.

oh-so-pretty fruit cones

- pearl dust in one or two colours
  (from baking supply shops)
- 1 tablespoon water
- pastry brush
- waffle cones
- fresh fruit

Place half a teaspoon of pearl dust in a small dish. Add a little water at a time until you get a slightly runny paste. Use a pastry brush to paint your cones. Fill with fruit just before serving.

watermelon glasses

- double-sided sticky tape
- mason jars
- green twine
- black marker pen
- strawberry milk

Use tape to attach the green twine to the bottom third of the jar by wrapping it around tightly, then draw 'seeds' on to make these cute watermelon glasses. Fill with strawberry milk.

cake

red velvet cake

Make the two red velvet cakes on page 214.

orange cream cheese icing

- 500 g (1 lb 2 oz) cream cheese, at room temperature
- 120 g (4½ oz) butter, unsalted, at room temperature
- 1 teaspoon vanilla extract
- 300 g (10½ oz/3 cups) icing (confectioners') sugar, sifted
- 1 teaspoon orange zest
- 1 teaspoon milk (if needed)
- nigella, cornflowers or borage, to decorate (see page 208)

Serves 12–14

Beat the cream cheese and butter until just smooth. Stir through the vanilla, then add the sifted icing sugar a half cup at a time until combined. Stir through the zest. Taste test time. If the icing is a little too thick add a teaspoon of milk.

Pipe the icing onto the cake's bottom layer. Leave a finger width to the edge because the weight of the top layer will push the icing out to the edge. Go around the edge with the piping bag again to fill it out, then pipe icing onto the cake's top layer and garnish with flowers before serving.

party favours

additional ideas

felt acorns (page 125); bookmarks (page 191); matchbox treasure (page 169) filled with cute little erasers

dotty popcorn favour boxes

• plain paper

• washi tape (various colours/patterns)

• 4 cm (1½ in) holepunch

• popcorn boxes

Stick the various washi tapes onto the plain paper one atop the other in horizontal lines until the band formed is slightly wider than your holepunch.

Punch out circles, peel the paper off the back, then stick onto the popcorn boxes.

little kitty friend

• small tin or box

• felt in two different colours

• red and black embroidery thread

• sequins

• stuffing

• hot glue gun

• fabric scraps for the bed

Choose a tin or box that will fit your felt kitty nicely. Cut the felt shapes according to the template on page 217. Sew a nose and mouth onto the muzzle with black thread. Sew eyes onto the face – position them at the centre horizontally. Line up the top of the nose with the eyes. Place a tiny bit of stuffing into the muzzle, then sew it onto the face. Add whiskers with black thread. Position the ears. Use blanket stitch to sew from one ear all the way around the face to the other ear (there are excellent tutorials on embroidery stitches online if you need to brush up on your needlework knowledge). Fill with stuffing and sew closed.

Sew two sequins onto the dress front. Position the legs and arms and sew from one arm all the way around to the other arm using blanket stitch, leaving the top open. Fill with stuffing and sew closed. Use hot glue to attach the head to the body and the tail to the back of the dress. Last, make a comfy bed for your kitty in the tin or box from pretty fabric scraps.

treasure jars

• small glass jars with corks

• glitter and coloured twine

Fill little glass jars with glitter. Decorate with twine.

cardboard
box

is there anything a cardboard box can't do?

Hooray for the cardboard box. Children the world over play with them, cats like to hide in them and they are endlessly full of opportunities. This is a great birthday party for creative little people (and adults). Please remember to recycle this party when you've finished with it.

decorations

You can do so many cool things with cardboard that the problem will be narrowing it down to just a few. You can decorate with all sorts of cardboard garlands cut into different shapes, or make cardboard animals or plants and place them around the house.

box stack

- boxes in different shapes and sizes

Make a huge pile of your cardboard boxes. The children will know exactly what to do. Simply stand back and behold. This is a great icebreaker to start the party.

cardboard garland

- cardboard
- black marker pen
- paint in various colours
- thread
- sewing machine

Cut diamond shapes from cardboard (don't worry if they aren't all uniform in size). Decorate them with paint and markers as you please, then run them through your sewing machine to connect them into a garland (see the image opposite; I recommend using a denim needle).

DIY cardboard cactus

- cardboard
- pencil
- Stanley knife
- cutting mat
- paints in various colours
- black marker pen
- 3 terracotta pots in various sizes
- scoria (from garden supply stores)

These cute cactus friends are based on a design by the super-talented Brittany Watson Jepsen of The House that Lars Built. For the complete instructions and free templates see thehousethatlarsbuilt.com and search cardboard cactus.

Using the templates as a guide, trace some basic cactus shapes on the cardboard. The main thing is to make sure the pieces are going to slot into each other.

Cut out the shapes with a Stanley knife or scissors. You'll have three sets of pieces – one for each cactus type. Make sure they fit into each other and make any niggly adjustments if you need to.

Paint one set of leaves green and two sets white. Or mix it up a bit.

When the pieces are completely dry, use the black marker pen to draw patterns on the leaves, then slot them together.

Now to plant them. Cover the pot hole at the bottom of each terracotta pot with a piece of cardboard. Position your cactus in the pot and get a helpful soul to carefully pour the scoria around the cactus. Give the pot a gentle wiggle to make sure it's stable – you might need to add a little more scoria.

Dang, they're so cute.

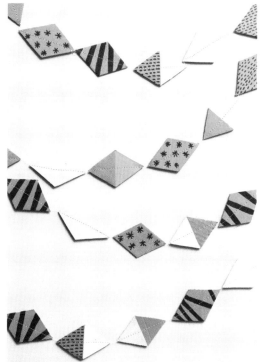

activities

box maze

- large cardboard boxes of roughly the same size
- double-sided sticky tape or washi tape

You can make this maze as big or small, or as complicated or simple, as you want (space willing!). You'll need large cardboard boxes of roughly the same size. Retail stores that sell TVs, microwaves and other appliances will have plenty of these. Just ask and they will direct you to the correct recycling dumpster.

To make the maze, place your boxes next to each other to fit the space you want to use. You can connect the boxes with double-sided sticky tape or washi tape to prevent them from sliding apart. Then go through and select where you want to cut internal walls within the maze. The doorways should all be roughly the same size so that they are easy to crawl through. See the illustration on page 160 for set-up inspiration.

cardboard animal painting

- card in various colours
- paint and brushes
- marker pens and glitter
- glue sticks

Cut various animal shapes from card ahead of time.

Set up a table with the paints, markers and everything else needed and ask the children to decorate the animals. While the beasties are drying, the children can work on their new home in the wonderful Box City.

creating Box City

- cardboard boxes of roughly the same size
- sticky tape
- pretty wrapping paper or scraps of old wallpaper, for backgrounds
- coloured card
- cut-out shapes including trees, doors and windows
- multiple glue sticks and tape dispensers
- marker pens
- fairy lights to pin to the wall behind the city (optional)

All those little critters the kids made are going to need a home, so it's time to make Box City. This is a group project. I'd suggest decorating one or two individual boxes in the city just to get the kids' imaginations fired up. This activity will likely take up a fair bit of time but the kids will love it.

Prepare by creating a multi-level city: stack the boxes on top of each other and connect them with tape (see the top image).

Now let the kids select backgrounds for the boxes and items to add to each individual 'room' in the city: furniture, greenery, animals, flowers ... there are no limits. Use glue and tape to stick everything into place.

When the city is complete you can turn on the fairy lights. Yeah!

cardboard crowns

- craft paper
- tape
- marker pens
- glitter
- glue
- little sticker gems

The above activities are probably all you'll have time for in a 90-minute party, but you can have this activity ready to go just in case.

Pre-cut crowns in various shapes, supply the tools to decorate and let the kids at it.

additional ideas
make a box marble run;
make box feet from old tissue
boxes; knock-over-the-box-
tower with a tennis ball

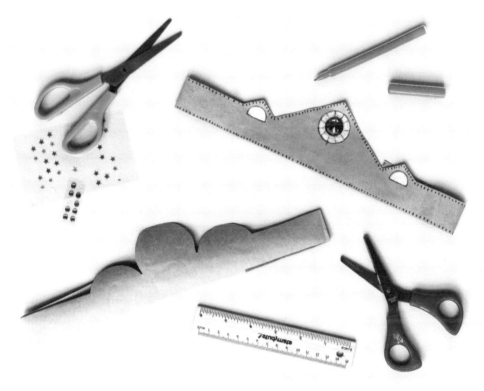

food

The food for this party is all about the packaging, but it still should be tasty and appealing. Make food parcels for each child using the suggestions below (and add in any extra goodies). Make sure the boxes you are using for the food parcels are going to be big enough to accommodate everything. Tie twine around the full boxes (use the same colour as on the cake). The beauty of these boxes is that they can be put together ahead of time.

bespoke bread rolls

- bread rolls
- various fillings
- waxed paper
- twine

Make up a variety of bread rolls and wrap them in parchment or waxed paper and tie with twine. When you're ready to make up the kids' lunch boxes ask them to choose which type of roll they'd like in their pack.

cupcake case fruit tubs

- blueberries, strawberries
- fancy cupcake cases
- eco-wooden forks (from party supply shops)

Fill with blueberries, strawberries or other cut fruit. You could buy some eco-wooden forks to complete the look, or just pop in some small forks from your kitchen.

pretzel pack

- chocolate-dipped pretzels (page 188)
- 5 cardboard cylinders or toilet rolls
- coloured twine

Makes 5

Cut the cylinders or toilet rolls to the length you want. Cover one end with craft paper using sticky tape to hold it in place, then cover the sides with paper. Tie some pretty twine around the cylinder and pop the chocolate-coated pretzels inside.

muffins-a-go-go

- 12 muffin cases
- 220 g (8 oz/1½ cups) self-raising flour (or use 220 g all-purpose flour with 1½ teaspoons salt and 3 teaspoons baking soda)
- 115 g (4 oz/½ cup) caster (superfine) sugar
- 250 ml (8½ fl oz/1 cup) buttermilk
- 125 ml (4 fl oz/½ cup) vegetable oil
- 1 egg, lightly whisked
- 1 teaspoon vanilla extract
- ¾ cup raspberries

Makes 12

Preheat the oven to 180°C (350°F). Place the muffin cases into a muffin tray.

Mix the dry ingredients together in a large bowl. Use a large jug to measure and mix the buttermilk, vegetable oil and egg. When well combined stir through the vanilla and raspberries.

Gently fold the wet ingredients into the dry ingredients using a spatula. It's ready when just combined.

Spoon the mixture into the cases and place in the preheated oven. Bake for 20–25 minutes, until golden on top.

bottles & paper straws

- small drink bottles
- twine
- paper straws

The drinks will be the last thing you place in the boxes. Make sure the lids are on securely, then tie a bit of twine around the top of the bottle in a bow.

cake

chocolate box cake

Make the easy chocolate cake on
page 213, using a 23 cm (9 in) square
cake tin.

- white fondant (see page 207)
- letter cookie cutters (or a piping bag
  if you are confident with writing on
  cakes)
- red gel paste food colour
- half batch of chocolate Swiss
  meringue buttercream (page 206)

decoration

- twine

Serves 16

Roll out the white fondant and make a rectangle large enough for the birthday child's name
and address. Use the letter stamp to personalise to your child. Make a little batch of red
fondant and make a long, thin rectangle. Stamp 'FRAGILE' on this label. Store until you are
ready to decorate.

When the cake is cool cut the top off the cake with a long serrated knife so that it is level.
Cut the sides straight to form nice sharp, boxy edges. Now you can pop it in the refrigerator
or freezer.

When you are ready to ice, make the chocolate Swiss meringue buttercream and do a
crumb coat (page 204). Chill the cake in the refrigerator, then do the final coat. Run your
knife or spatula under very hot water, then dry it. Use the knife to make the icing as smooth
and level as possible and try to keep the edges sharp. Chill again.

When the cake has chilled, cut four long pieces of the twine. Poke the pieces of twine under
the cake on opposite sides of the cake. Now gently pull the pieces up together over the cake
and tie a bow.

Pop on the fondant labels just before serving.

party favours

additional ideas
alien key ring (page 111);
bookmarks (page 191);
lollipop disguises (page 203)

cardboard favour boxes

- small boxes
- brown craft paper
- coloured twine
- balloons, pompoms etc. to decorate

Collect small boxes of various sizes (hint: go on a raid of the recycling bin). Put your favours inside, then wrap the boxes in brown paper and dress them up with pretty bibs and bobs: balloons, pompoms, washi tape spots (page 159) and anything else you can think of.

cardboard necklaces/badges

- cardboard
- black marker pen
- twine
- sticky tape
- hot glue gun and brooch fasteners (optional)

Simple but cute. Cut shapes from cardboard and draw patterns on them with black marker. Attach them to twine with sticky tape to make a necklace. To make a badge, hot glue brooch fasteners on the back of the cut-outs or fasten them to clothing with tape.

matchbox treasure

- craft matchboxes
- pretty paper
- glue (the kind that dries clear)
- clear gems
- little googly eyes

Glue pretty paper around a craft matchbox. You can fill these little treasure boxes with anything you like but for these ones I've added little gem friends. Glue the bottom of your gem and stick it on some patterned paper. Wait until it has dried before cutting closely around the base. Add eyes.

TOXIC
HAZARD

science

explore science with experiments galore

A science party can seem daunting, but you don't need a PhD in bioscience to pull this party together. There are heaps of really simple, cool science activities that you can do at home. (There are also companies that specialise in running science parties for kids if you want to outsource.)

Sr
87.62

Y
88.906

Al
26.982

Si
28.086

Ge
72.61

decorations

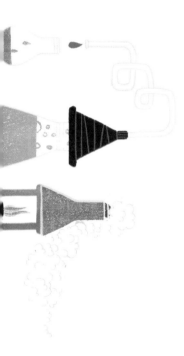

To set up for this party I recommend you harness your inner geek, put on a lab coat and break out the baking soda and vinegar. Add an atom mobile or two – who knew atoms could be so cute?

felt ball atom mobile

- memory wire (necklace size)
- 5 small felt balls
- 1 large felt ball
- invisible thread
- hot glue gun

Use the memory wire to make three large circles of the same size. Using the image opposite as a guide, thread the small felt balls (electrons) onto the wires and position roughly in place. Use hot glue to stick the wires together – another adult is helpful here to hold everything in place while you glue. Now use invisible thread to suspend the nucleus (a larger felt ball) within the electron cloud.

chalkboard backdrop

- chalkboard
- chalk

To set the scene, use a chalkboard as your cake table backdrop. You can get chalkboards in various sizes from craft stores.

Decorate with your favourite scientific formulae.

$m = m_0\sqrt{1-\frac{v^2}{c^2}}$
$E = m_0c^2 + \frac{mv^2}{2}$
P(x)
$F = G\frac{M_1M_2}{R^2}$
20
$r_n = 4\pi\varepsilon_0 n^2 n^2$

activities

Don't wait until party day to try out these experiments. Have a practice beforehand to make sure they all run smoothly and you know what to expect.

lava lamps

- 3 bottles (old soft drink bottles are perfect) with lids
- water
- vegetable oil
- eyedropper
- liquid food colouring in three colours
- dissolvable aspirin or Alka-Seltzer

Pour water into the bottles until they are one third full. Pour in the oil until it is 6 cm (2½ in) from the top of the bottle. The oil will sit on top of the water because water is heavier than oil. Using an eyedropper, add a different colour food dye to each bottle. The food colour will form little balls that slowly descend through the oil layer – because they, too, are heavier than oil – until they reach the water, where they will disperse.

Now for the really fun bit. Break the aspirin into quarters and drop it into each bottle. The science behind this experiment is down to good old CO_2. When the Aspro reaches the coloured water sitting at the bottom of the bottle it creates CO_2 bubbles, which will float up through the oil until they reach the top and 'pop' before sinking down to the water layer at the bottom of the bottle. On and on it goes. Until it runs out of CO_2. That's when it's time to put the lid on and keep it for next time.

tornado in a jar

- large glass jar with a lid
- water
- 2 teaspoons dishwashing liquid
- 5 drops of liquid food colouring
- good pinch of glitter

Pour water into the jar until it's about three-quarters full. Add the dishwashing liquid, then the food colouring and a pinch of glitter. Pop the lid on nice and tight.

Hold the jar and slowly start swirling it in a narrow circle until a mini-tornado starts to form. The water right next to the glass is pulled along when you swirl the jar, but the water further near the middle of the jar takes longer to react to the friction. When you stop swirling the jar, the water closest to the glass will react first, while the inner water will keep spinning for a few seconds longer.

activities

additional ideas

check these out on Google or YouTube: magic tea bag rocket; elephant toothpaste; hot air balloon bottle

cloud in a jar

- boiling water
- thick-walled glass jar
- ice cubes
- plate that fits securely over the jar opening (right way up)
- packet of matches

Pour boiling water into the jar to 5 cm (2 in) deep and swirl it around to warm the sides. Put several ice cubes on the plate and put the plate on top of the jar. Wait 30 seconds then swiftly remove the plate and drop in a lighted match before putting the plate with the ice back on top. Within a few seconds a cloud will form.

While you have the cloud trapped, you can explain the science behind cloud formation (your two minutes start now). The moist air (water vapour) created by the hot water sticks to the smoke particles. When it comes into contact with cold air (through the ice) it condenses into itty-bitty cloud droplets. Has it been two minutes? Release the cloud and watch it float away.

Mentos geyser

- diet cola
- 1 mint Mentos

Unless you want your house to be completely covered with sticky cola I'd suggest you do this outside – or even better, take it to the local park.

Get the children to stand well back. Open the cola, pop the Mentos in and – this is very important, so listen up – run away very fast. Foamy soda is going to shoot up into the air. Some folks advocate a 2-litre bottle and 7 Mentos because this causes the biggest reaction. I'll let you judge how far you want to experiment with this.

egg in a bottle

- glass bottle
- packet of matches or a lighter
- small piece of paper
- hard-boiled egg, peeled

You'll need a glass bottle with an opening that is slightly smaller than the egg's diameter.

Light the piece of paper and drop it into the bottle. Quickly place the egg over the bottle's opening. Watch it getting sucked in.

So what's happening? If you put an egg on top of a bottle the air pressure within the bottle and outside the bottle is the same. But if you place a burning piece of paper in the bottle it will heat the air up inside the bottle causing the molecules to expand and take up more room. The fire in the paper uses up all the oxygen in the bottle and the flame goes out, then the bottle cools down again. What happens when the air cools down? That's right, the molecules move closer together and therefore the cool air takes up less space. Now the pressure outside of the bottle is greater than the pressure inside the bottle, causing an imbalance. And that pesky egg is in the way. The air pressure from outside the bottle becomes so strong that it pushes the egg into the bottle.

Now you just have to figure out how to get your egg out of the bottle.

food

radioactive bagels

- bagels
- cheese slices, cut into rounds the same size as the bagel
- ham, cut into triangles
- cherry tomatoes, halved

Cut the bagels in half. Place a round slice of cheese on a bagel half and top it with three pieces of ham to resemble a radiation warning sign. Finish by positioning half a cherry tomato in the centre.

make a fruit molecule

- blueberries
- raspberries
- rock melon, carved into balls
- mini marshmallows
- toothpicks

Join blueberries, raspberries, strawberries and mini marshmallows using toothpicks to create these build-you-own fruit molecules.

jelly beakers

- 85g (3 oz) jelly (Jell-0) crystals
- 8 small (100 ml/3½ fl oz) glasses or beakers (from party supply or bargain shops)
- 200 ml (7 fl oz) cream, for whipping
- 8 plastic syringes (50 ml/1¾ fl oz; available at pharmacies)

Makes 8

Make the jelly following the packet instructions and pour it into glasses or beakers to set. Next, whisk the cream using an electric mixer on high speed until soft peaks form. When the jelly has set, top it with whipped cream. Draw up extra whipped cream into syringes and place on top.

sweet DNA

- licorice straps
- jubes
- toothpicks

Impale the jubes on toothpicks and sandwich between the licorice straps.

explosive spiders

- cordial
- vanilla ice cream
- lemonade (lemon-lime soda)

Pour about 2 cm (1 in) of cordial into the bottom of a glass, then scoop spoonfuls of ice cream on top. Pour in the lemonade and watch it foam. You could serve these in beakers or conical flasks for extra science points. Be sure to supply straws.

cake

'the rats have taken over the laboratory' cake

Make the easy chocolate cake recipe on page 213 and bake it in a 23 cm (9 in) round cake tin.

- white buttercream (page 205)
- ganache drip icing (page 207)
- food colouring of your choice

decoration

- beaker and/or flask (from party supply or bargain shops)
- small toy rats (optional)
- fondant (optional; see page 207)

Serves 16

Make a batch of buttercream and, once the cake has cooled, do a crumb coat (page 204), then finish with a second coat. Position a beaker, conical flask or test tube onto the buttercream icing while it is gooey and set it to harden in the refrigerator.

Make a batch of ganache and add colour. Take your well-chilled cake from the refrigerator and use a spoon to dribble the ganache over the side of the cake where you want to create the spillage. Use a funnel to pour ganache into the beaker. Dribble some ganache down the side of the beaker. Finally, join up the spillage from the beaker to the side of the cake where it has spilled over. Go slowly. You can always add more.

Add a lab rat or two. You could make your own rats from fondant, or simply use any ratty friends you have hanging around.

party favours

additional ideas

edible green slime (heaps of recipes on the internet); edible moon rocks (from cake decorating shops); alien key rings (page 111)

molecule favour bag

- coloured card
- glue
- brown party bags
- black marker pen
- coloured twine

When it's time to say goodbye to your party guests, give them a good dose of science fun to take home. Create sciency favour bags by gluing round cardboard cut-outs onto brown party bags. Connect the shapes with black marker and you have a molecule! Close the bags by threading some twine through the top.

test tube treats

- plastic test tubes
- small sweets

These slim plastic test tubes with corks are available from party supply stores. Fill with sweet treats of your choice.

marshmallow poppers

- small plastic cups
- balloons
- small marshmallows (or little felt balls)

Cut off the bottom third of each cup. Tie your balloon in a knot and cut off about half a centimetre (¼ in) from the other end – you want to be able to stretch the balloon to fit over the top of the cup. A little give and take may be needed depending on the sturdiness of your cup. Place your projectile of choice on the balloon's knot on the inside of the cup. To fire, you need to pull back on the knot from the outside. Instant mayhem.

optical illusions

- prints of optical illusions
- envelopes

There are heaps of terrific optical illusions on the internet, including free printables. Print up a selection of them and pop them in an envelope.

glamping

camping – but without the mosquitos & mud

A glamping sleepover is a really special way for older kids to celebrate their birthday. Or – if you're feeling game – younger children will be thrilled to have their first sleepover party.

decorations

Bring the harsh outdoors inside with style: bespoke tents, felt fireplaces, snuggly blankets, cute craft activities and s'mores galore.

A-frame tents

These gorgeous little A-frame tents are so cosy the kids will never want to sleep anywhere else. You'll find tutorials online to make these simple tents, which is a great idea if you want to make just one or two that you can keep and reuse. However, if you need a few tents I'd recommend hiring them (and it won't cost much more than buying all the materials to make them). There are companies that specialise in hiring out tents (with accompanying mattresses and other goodies) and they come in lots of different fabrics so you can colour coordinate your decorations (if you're into that kind of thing ...).

felt camp fire

• red felt
• orange felt
• sticks
• hot glue gun

Cut red and orange flame shapes from felt using the image opposite as a guide and use hot glue to bind them. Arrange the flames amongst some strategically placed sticks.

night lights

• glass jars with lids
• glow sticks

Create a night light for each party-goer by putting a glow stick in a pretty glass jar and filling with water (the water will make the light more shimmery). Screw the lid on tight.

activities

DIY felt ball garlands

- small felt balls in various colours (around 20 for each child)
- embroidery thread
- embroidery needles
- small beads (optional)

This is an easy and inexpensive activity and the children will have fun making these garlands to decorate their tents. Show them how to thread the felt balls on, then tie a knot so they don't slide around. Have lots of different colours available so they can improvise. You could do this with pompoms instead (but have the pompoms ready to go or they'll be there all night).

god's eye

- short sturdy sticks of approximately the same length
- yarn in several colours

You might want to get the kids started by securely tying the two sticks together in the middle to form a cross – but older kids should be fine with this.

Start by wrapping the yarn around one of the sticks in a clockwise direction, starting in the centre of the cross. Move to the next stick in a counter-clockwise direction, but wrap the yarn clockwise around the stick. Keep working around the frame in a counter-clockwise direction, but wrapping clockwise around each individual stick, until all sticks are full. Tie a knot around the last stick. On one side, the yarn will be flat, on the other side, you can see where it wraps around the sticks.

If you get stuck, you can always check out YouTube!

make your own bath bombs

- 120 g (4 oz/1 cup) Epsom salts, ground to a fine texture
- 220 g (8 oz/2 cups) bicarbonate of soda (baking soda)
- 120 g (4 oz/1 cup) cornflour (cornstarch)
- 120 g (4 oz/1 cup) citric acid
- 2–2½ teaspoons water
- 2 teaspoons essential oil (lavender, orange or peppermint are all good)
- 3 teaspoons olive oil
- drop or two of food colouring (have a few options available)
- 5 small bowls (one for each child)
- bath bomb moulds (alternatively, you can use cupcake cases or muffin tins)

optional extras

- glitter, confetti – you can sprinkle a little in the base of the mould before you pack in the mixture so that it will look pretty from the outside
- herbal tea – cut open the bag of your favourite herbal tea and dump the contents in the mix
- dried rose petals or lavender

Makes five bath bombs, depending on the size of your moulds.

Bath bombs are super easy to make. The kids will love making their own unique combinations of scents and textures, so have a few ideas up your sleeve.

Epsom salts are quite coarse, so I run them through the food processor for a few seconds to make them finer – but feel free to skip this step if you want.

Whisk together all the dry ingredients in a large bowl until well combined.

Mix the wet ingredients together in a separate bowl.

Slowly add the wet to the dry, whisking all the time. If it starts to fizz, slow down. When it's all combined you'll have a lovely, sweet smelling bowl of crumble. If you pick up a handful and squeeze, it should clump together nicely.

Divide the mixture between five smaller bowls so that each child can add their choice of extras. When it is time to press the bath bombs into shape, get the kids to firmly pack part of the mix into one side of the bath bomb mould, leaving a little mound on top. Next, tell them to fill the other side of the mould and push the two halves tightly together before gently lifting one half of the mould off – if it collapses, don't worry, just repeat the previous steps. Leave the other half of the mould on the bath bombs for now and place them onto a tray. Put the tray into the refrigerator for a couple of hours (it's much easier to remove the mould when it has been chilled).

Retrieve from the refrigerator, very gently take the other side of the mould off and allow to dry on a folded-up towel covered with baking paper (parchment) or foil. They'll continue to dry out and be ready to go home with the kids in the morning.

additional ideas
get the kids to make some chatterboxes
with 'truth or dare' messages; watch a
favourite movie; arm them with torches and
take them on a night-time walk around the
neighbourhood. If you happen to have one
of those nifty Instax cameras let the kids
borrow it for the evening – they'll have a
blast taking photos of each other.

food

glamping snacks

....

campfire s'mores cones

- waffle cones
- Nutella
- peanut butter
- marshmallows
- raspberries
- dark chocolate, roughly chopped

If you're having a real campfire you can really go to town with these waffle cones. Fill with your choice of Nutella, peanut butter, marshmallows, raspberries, chocolate and more. Wrap in foil and place upright in the fire briefly. And if you don't have a campfire, don't worry, pop them into an oven preheated to 180°C (350°F) for 8–10 minutes. Remember to keep them upright.

marshmallow sticks

- marshmallows
- sticks
- melting chocolate

You don't need a campfire for these tasty marshmallow snacks: it's all in the presentation. Simply impale the marshmallows on sticks and dip them in melted chocolate. Let the chocolate dry before gathering the sticks at the top and tying in a teepee shape with twine.

chocolate pretzels

- 40 pretzels
- 100 g (3½ oz) chocolate, melted
- sprinkles

Serves 5

Dip the pretzels in the melted chocolate then the sprinkles – you can use a variety of coloured sprinkles – and leave to set. Just the thing for when you're working hard on a felt garland.

dinner

....

Older kids will probably want to choose their favourite dinner but you can still glamp-up the table with a little glamour: fresh flowers, pretty glasses, candles, bespoke lemonade (lemon-lime soda) infusions (see page 122) and raspberry tea.

waffle station

....

waffles

- 300 g (10½ oz/2 cups) plain (all-purpose) flour
- 2 teaspoons baking powder
- 80 g (2¾ oz/⅓ cup) caster (superfine) sugar
- 100 g (3½ oz) butter, unsalted
- 2 eggs
- 500 ml (17 fl oz/2 cups) milk
- waffle iron

condiments & co.

- maple syrup, cream and ice cream, fresh fruit, crushed nuts, Nutella, lemon and sugar
- fresh orange juice

Nothing beats freshly made waffles for breakfast.

Combine the flour, baking powder and sugar in a large mixing bowl. Melt the butter and let it cool a little before mixing through the flour. Lightly whisk the eggs and then stir into the mixture. Slowly stir through the milk.

Let it rest for an hour before cooking as per your waffle maker's instructions.

Offer a selection of condiments and don't forget the freshly squeezed orange juice.

Nom, nom. Waffle so good.

cake

'pretty in pink' triple-layer sponge cake

Make one and a half times the quantity
for the sponge cake on page 212 and bake
it in three round cake tins
(20 cm x 5 cm/8 in x 2 in).

• 200 ml (7 fl oz) cream, for whipping
• basic icing recipe (page 205) with
  raspberry flavouring

decoration

• fresh flowers (page 208)

Serves 12

To make the whipped cream for the filling, using an electric mixer on high speed, whisk the
cream until stiff peaks form.

When the sponge cakes have cooled, pipe the whipped cream around the centre of the
layers using a star tip. Don't go closer than a finger width to the edge because the weight
of the top layers will squash the cream out. When you have stacked up the layers go back
around the cake with the star tip and tidy it up.

Make the icing and drizzle it over the top of the cake. When it has set, smother the top of the
cake with fresh flowers.

A cake stand is a must for this cake – it would feel naked without it.

party favours

additional ideas
matchbox treasure
(page 169) filled with cute
little erasers; marshmallow
poppers (page 181);
strawberry friends
(page 149)

furoshiki favour boxes

- small boxes
- colourful fabric

These boxes will be greeted with much excitement when they are discovered waiting at the opening of each tent. Furoshiki is a traditional Japanese wrapping cloth used to wrap and carry goods. Any pretty fabric will do, although lightweight fabric is better. For a small rectangle box you'll need around 70 cm (27 in) square of fabric. Fill with pretty soaps, delicious organic chocolate, paper cranes and more, but make sure to leave room for the bath bomb.

felt bracelet & necklace

- darning needle
- felt balls – 1 cm (½ in) and 2 cm (¾ in)
- elastic thread (allow about 16 cm/ 6¼ in per bracelet)
- small packet of memory wire (necklace size)

Use the needle to thread the 1 cm (½ in) felt balls onto elastic thread for the bracelet; you'll need around 10 per bracelet. Thread two of the 1 cm (½ in) felt balls and three of the 2 cm (¾ in) felt balls onto the memory wire to make the necklace.

animal bookmarks

- origami paper
- pretty coloured paper
- black marker pen

Origami paper is the perfect size for creating these nifty bookmarks. Use the template on page 220 to cut out the main part of the bookmark, then create ears and paws from pretty paper and glue them on. Finally, draw on some cute faces.

super sleuth

solving mysteries in style

There are many different ways to throw a mystery party: you can download a free 'mystery party package' from the internet with ready-made clues and story line, or you can simply arm the kids with torches and send them outside in the dark and they'll make their own fun. Older kids will love a detailed 'case' to solve with a story structure and characters to play. For younger kids, you could pose a simple mystery such as 'the missing party favours'. Either way, there is plenty of scope to create a super fun and creative party tailored to your child.

decorations

We're channelling classic detective series for this look: Nancy Drew meets Sherlock Holmes in a tweed bonanza. Think 1940s, newsprint, typewriters and intrigue ... plenty of intrigue.

newsprint garland

- 4 cm (1½ in) holepunch
- old book you don't want
- card in 2 or 3 colours
- thread
- sewing machine

Use the holepunch to punch out circles from the book and coloured card. Pair up one card and one book circle.

Have a play with the tension on your sewing machine to make sure the stitches come out nice and even on the paper. Connect the circles into a garland by sewing a straight line through the middle of each paired circle. Make sure you leave around 1 cm (½ in) space between each circle – this will allow the garland to move freely and hang nicely.

When you're happy with the length, lay the garland out and carefully fold each circle in half so that you create three-dimensional circles.

Multiple strands look good together, or run a long single strand in horizontal loops on a wall.

getting into character

- detective dress-ups and accessories

Supply accessories galore for your party guests and they'll be able to get into character. You'll need a few tweed or cloche hats, neck ties, hair bows, spectacles, assorted moustaches, leather handbags, magnifying glasses, notepads and pens.

photo booth

- large sheet of paper for the mugshot backdrop
- black and white card
- glue
- marker pens

Make a 'mug shot' photo booth – rule up heights on large format white paper and stick it to the wall. Create name cards by cutting black card squares and gluing white card strips on top. Write down each kid's name with black marker pen (see the photos on page 197). Ask each child to hold up their name card when they have their picture taken. This will make a terrific memento.

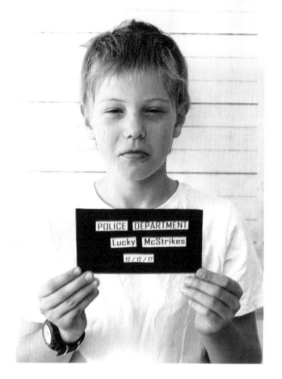

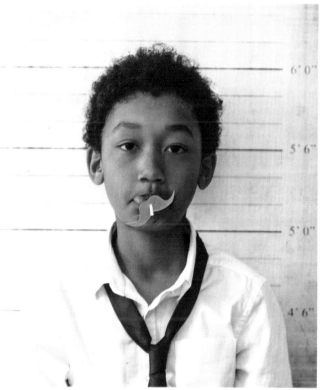

activities

Regardless of the kind of mystery theme you choose, you're going to need to supply clues for the kids to solve the crime. One clue should lead to the next clue, and then the next until the solution is revealed. Try to vary the type of clues, and don't make them too hard to solve.

clue #1

- 2 sheets of thin paper
- pencil

For your first clue, type up a statement about the crime on the first sheet of paper. Your clue will be hidden inside the statement.

Let's say your clue is: 'on the doormat'. Go through the statement and find the clue's letters in the correct order (you'd start with o, then move on to n and so forth). Layer the blank sheet of paper over the paper containing the statement and circle the letters on the blank piece of paper. The kids can read the clue by holding the two pieces of paper up to the light.

clue #2

- white pastel
- white paper
- lead pencil

For the next clue, write a secret message using a white pastel on white paper. Now hand write or print a misleading clue over the top of the pastel. The pastel will be nearly invisible to the eye.

Leave a lead pencil with the clue. You can even scribble a little bit of pencil on the clue to give the kids the idea: when they draw over the writing with the pencil the pastel clue will reveal itself.

clue #3

- cardboard
- coloured pencils

This is a puzzle jumble clue. Write or draw the clue on cardboard and then cut the card into shapes. Jumble them up and place in an envelope for the kids to reassemble.

clue #4

- paper or flash cards
- pen

Create a cipher for the kids to decode a scrambled clue.

Assign each letter of the alphabet a new letter and create a card that holds the code. Next, write a message in the secret alphabet on a separate card. Give the codebreaker card to the young detectives and let them figure out what the clue says.

clue #5

- Stanley knife
- old book you don't want

If this is the final clue in your party, this is where you'll reveal where the goodies are hidden (or otherwise resolve your mystery). Use a Stanley knife to cut a hole in the pages of a hardcover book and hide the final clue inside. The children should be directed to find the book in the previous clue.

food

savoury pastries

- cheese and spinach triangles
- cheese twists
- mini quiches
- pesto scrolls

Pick up a selection of your child's favourite savoury pastries from your local bakery. Delicate cheese and spinach filo triangles, cheese twists, dainty mini quiches and pesto scrolls make great finger food.

chocolate brownies

- 310 g (11 oz/1⅓ cups) caster (superfine) sugar
- 110 g (4 oz/¾ cup) plain (all-purpose) flour, sifted
- 30 g (1 ¼oz/¼ cup) Dutch (unsweetened) cocoa powder, sifted
- 3 eggs, whisked
- 1 teaspoon vanilla extract
- 125 g (4½ oz) unsalted butter
- 125 g (4½ oz) dark chocolate

Makes 16

A must for hungry detectives.

Preheat your oven to 180°C (350°F). Grease a 20 cm (8 in) square cake tin and line with baking paper (parchment).

Pour the sugar into a medium bowl and add the flour and cocoa. Combine the eggs and vanilla and add to the dry ingredients.

Stir the butter and chocolate together over a double boiler until melted. Allow to cool a little before quickly mixing through the remaining ingredients. Pour the batter into the tin and bake for around 30 minutes – if you poke a skewer into the centre it should come out slightly gooey. Let it cool completely before turning out and slicing into rectangles. Store in an airtight container.

cinnamon donuts

- donuts from your favourite outlet

Everyone knows that detectives need donuts to do their best work so I suggest you stock up.

sleuth juice

- fake moustaches
- holepunch
- straws

Use card to make moustaches in a variety of shapes (see templates on page 219), then punch a hole in the centre with a holepunch and slide them onto a straw. Serve with your juice of choice.

cake

time bomb cake

Double the quantity of the pound cake recipe on page 215 to make two half-spheres of cake in a 20 cm (8 in) ball cake tin.

- white fondant (see page 207)
- letter cutters
- chocolate Swiss meringue buttercream (page 206)
- super black gel paste food colour

decoration
- sparkler candle

Serves 12–16

First, make fondant letters to go on the cake. Alternatively, if you're brave enough to pipe directly onto the cake you can do that when you ice the cake.

Make the pound cake recipe as per the instructions on page 215, but remember you're making two cakes, each a half sphere.

Make a batch of chocolate Swiss meringue buttercream. Stir through the super black gel food paste (you definitely need to use paste and not liquid colour here, or you'll alter the consistency of the buttercream) until you are happy with the colour.

Fetch your two half spheres of cake and cut each level across the bottom. Put them together to see how they fit. Make any adjustments if necessary. Place each half sphere flat side down on the bench and do a crumb coat (page 204) on each and chill. When chilled, place one half sphere upside-down in a small bowl or ramekin (for support) and apply a liberal amount of buttercream to the flat side. Now place your other half sphere on top and use buttercream to secure them together nicely. Apply buttercream to the top half of the ball. Chill briefly before turning the ball over and icing the other side. When it's nice and even, apply the fondant letters (or pipe letters) with a dab of buttercream.

Remember to serve your little 'bomb' with a sparkler candle!

party favours

additional ideas
magnifying glass;
notebooks; pocket torch

sleuth favour bags

- paper party bags
- old newspaper
- card in colour of choice
- glue
- paper doily
- small woooden pegs

Cut out round shapes from card or use leftovers from the newspaper garland (page 194). Glue newspaper onto the outside of simple paper party bags, then glue the card pieces onto the front. Add a paper doily cut to size on top and close the bag with a wooden peg.

lollipop disguises

- coloured card
- lollipops

Cut moustache shapes from coloured card (see templates on page 219); use a holepunch to put a hole in the centre and pop the moustaches onto lollipop sticks.

matchbox cameras

- craft matchboxes
- black paper
- glue
- grey card
- twine
- sticky tape

Cut the black paper into matchbox-width strips, long enough to wrap the entire matchbox. Glue onto the matchboxes. Add round and rectangular grey card cut-outs for the lens and buttons. Next, cut a long piece of twine and attach each end to the inside of the matchbox using tape.

Just what every detective needs for capturing important clues.

recipes & tips

freezing

All the cakes listed in this book freeze well except for the moon cake. To freeze, wrap the cooled cakes in two layers of plastic wrap and then a layer of foil. They'll keep well for up to two months.

crumb coat

For a professional look when icing a cake, you really need to do a 'crumb coat'. Think of it as priming the cake for the real icing. To crumb coat, put ¼ of the icing into a separate bowl (this is so you don't dirty all the icing with crumbs). Use a spatula (or the back of a bread knife) to cover the top and sides of the cake. You only need a thin covering and you'll probably be able to see the cake through the icing in some places.

Now pop the cake into the refrigerator for 30 minutes. Once chilled, you'll find applying the second layer of icing much easier and it will look much cleaner.

cake fail

Don't stress. It's probably not as bad as you think it is (we tend to be our own worst critics). And if it really is completely inedible, pop down to the local shops and pick up an ice cream cake. Everyone loves ice cream cake.

basic icing

....

- 125 g (4½ oz/1 cup) icing (confectioners') sugar
- 2–3 teaspoons full-cream (whole) milk
- dash of vanilla extract

Sift the icing sugar and stir in the milk and vanilla until you are happy with the consistency. Add food colouring if desired.

buttercream

....

- 250 g (9 oz) unsalted butter, cubed and at room temperature
- 1 teaspoon clear imitation vanilla extract
- 375 g (13 oz/3 cups) icing (confectioners') sugar
- 4 tablespoons full-cream (whole) milk

In a small bowl, beat the butter and vanilla until it becomes very pale (at least 5 minutes). Beat in the icing sugar and milk in two batches. Flavour and colour as desired. Store in an airtight container in the refrigerator for up to two weeks or freeze for up to two months. Before using, bring to room temperature and beat on slow speed until smooth.

When serving cakes that contain buttercream, always remove them from the refrigerator a couple of hours before the party – buttercream should be eaten at room temperature.

Swiss meringue buttercream

....

- 4 egg whites
- 225 g (1 cup /8 oz) caster (superfine) sugar
- pinch of salt
- 340 g (12 oz) butter, cubed and at room temperature
- 1 teaspoon clear imitation vanilla extract

Before starting, wipe down the inside of a large metal bowl with vinegar to remove any grease.

Whisk the egg whites and sugar in the bowl until combined. Place the bowl over a double boiler and whisk for around 3 minutes – until the meringue no longer feels grainy (the sugar should have melted).

Take off the heat and beat on high until stiff peaks form and the mixture has cooled to the touch. Don't proceed with the next step until it is at room temperature.

Add salt and slowly beat in the cubed butter a piece at a time. If the mixture separates, *don't panic*. It will be fine – increase the beating speed, continue adding the butter pieces and keep beating until it becomes smooth, light and delicious. This could be anywhere from 5 to 10 minutes (or more).

Mix through the vanilla or any other flavourings.

Store in an airtight container in the refrigerator for up to one week. Before using, bring to room temperature and beat on slow until smooth.

When serving cakes that contain buttercream, always remove them from the refrigerator a couple of hours before the party – buttercream should be eaten at room temperature.

chocolate Swiss meringue buttercream

....

Prepare the buttercream as per the above recipe, but omit the vanilla. Instead, melt 200 g (7 oz) of bittersweet chocolate and let it cool. After you have incorporated the butter, whisk in the chocolate.

colouring buttercream icing

....

Because buttercream is naturally a pale yellow colour you have to be careful when colouring. For instance, if you add blue food colouring you'll end up with green buttercream (yellow + blue = green). So if you're going to be adding colours to your buttercream, take it back to white first. *Don't* add white food colouring: add violet. I know, it seems weird. You're going to have to trust me on this one. If you require a true white buttercream add violet gel paste food colour. Use a toothpick to put the absolutely tiniest itty-bitty bit of the colour into the buttercream and mix through. Add more if necessary, going in tiny increments – if you take it too far you'll have purple icing.

fondant shapes

White fondant is readily available from supermarkets and cake supplies stores. You can also buy coloured fondant, but it's easy to colour it yourself. Knead gel paste food colour into the fondant until you are happy with the colour, then wrap it in plastic wrap and let it sit for a couple of days before using (the colour will intensify over that time). If you need a true black fondant I'd suggest buying it rather than colouring it, otherwise it can look a little flat.

If you are creating fondant shapes for your cake, it's best to let them dry out before placing them on buttercream icing. You can make the fondant shapes well before the party (months, in fact). Allow them to dry out before storing them in a cardboard box. This allows them to breathe – never put fondant in the refrigerator as it will go soft and sticky.

chocolate ganache

• one part double (heavy) cream
• one part white melting chocolate

Melt the cream and chocolate over a double boiler until lovely and smooth and drippy. Now is the time to colour with gel paste food colouring. Let it cool just a little before spooning it over your well-chilled cake. When you've finished decorating, pop the cake straight back in the refrigerator to set the ganache.

sugar syrup

• one part white sugar
• two parts water

To make the syrup, heat the water and sugar on the stovetop until the sugar has dissolved.

edible flowers

When using fresh flowers on cakes you can insert the flower stem into a lollipop stick and poke that into the cake to ensure the stem doesn't come into direct contact with the cake. If you want to place the flowers directly onto the cake, place a sheet of baking paper (parchment) where the flowers are going to go so they are not sitting directly on the icing. Never use florist flowers directly on a cake – you can't be sure what has been sprayed onto them – and never poke florist wire directly into a cake, insert it into a lollipop stick as it can be coated with lead or may even rust inside the cake if left too long.

The following flowers are edible, providing you are certain no sprays or foliar fertilisers have been used on them. If you're not sure, don't use it.

- apple blossom
- borage
- camellia
- carnation
- chive flowers
- cornflower
- dahlia
- fuchsia
- geranium
- hibiscus
- lavender
- lilac

- marigold
- nasturtium
- nigella
- pansy
- peony
- primrose
- rose
- salvia
- snap dragon
- thyme
- viola
- violet

violet

nigella

geranium

nasturtium

salvia

chive

white cake

··

Serves 20

This is the recipe I use when I want to create cakes that require strong colours.
The following quantities are for the six-layer rainbow cake.

- 420 g (15 oz/2¾ cups) plain (all-purpose) flour
- 1 tablespoon bicarbonate of soda (baking soda)
- ½ teaspoon salt
- 220 g (8 oz) unsalted butter, at room temperature
- 450 g (1 lb/2 cups) caster (superfine) sugar
- 5 egg whites, room temperature
- 1 teaspoon clear imitation vanilla extract
- 360 ml (12 fl oz/1⅓ cups) full-cream (whole) milk, room temperature
- gel paste food colour in: red, orange, lemon yellow, mint green,
  royal blue and violet

Preheat oven to 160°C (320°F). Grease six round 20 cm (8 in) cake tins with butter and line the bottoms with baking paper (parchment).

Sift the flour, bicarbonate of soda and salt into a large bowl.

In another large bowl beat the butter and sugar until light and fluffy and as pale as possible. Slowly beat in the egg whites and vanilla extract until combined.

Alternate stirring in the flour mixture and milk in two batches. The batter should be well combined.

Divide the batter equally between six bowls and whisk in the food colouring slowly until you are happy with the shades. As soon as you reach a colour you are happy with, stop. The cakes will taste bitter if you add too much food colouring.

Pour the individual batters into the prepared cake tins. Wrap the sides of the tins in a wet tea towel (dish towel), then cover the wet tea towel with foil. Pop in the oven (bake in batches if you need to) and bake for approximately 20 minutes. They're ready when a skewer inserted into the middle comes out clean.

Cool the cake tins on a wire rack for around 10 minutes before turning out the cakes and allowing to cool completely. Use a pastry brush to paint sugar syrup (page 207) onto the tops and sides of your cakes to prevent the naked sides from drying out.

These cakes can be stored in an airtight container or plastic wrap in the freezer for up to two months or in the refrigerator for several days.

Note the quantities for the 'Thar be Treasure' cake are listed on page 96. You'll need four round 20 cm (8 in) cake tins for that cake.

naked cakes

If you're baking a cake that is going to be presented naked you'll need to make sure the sides don't brown whilst baking. Wrap the sides of the pan in a wet tea towel (dish towel), then cover the wet tea towel with foil. I also suggest putting a dish of cold water in the bottom of your oven when you turn it on to preheat.

sponge cake

Serves 10

The quantity in this recipe will give you enough for two thick layers of sponge.

• 120 g (4½ oz/1 cup) cornflour (cornstarch)
• 4 teaspoons custard powder (or instant pudding mix)
• 1 teaspoon cream of tartar
• ½ teaspoon bicarbonate of soda (baking soda)
• 4 eggs, separated and at room temperature
• 160 g (6 oz/⅔ cup) caster (superfine) sugar

chocolate sponge
• Add 4 tablespoons Dutch (unsweetened) cocoa powder to the dry ingredients.

Preheat oven to 170°C (340°F). Grease and line two 20 cm x 5 cm (8 in x 2 in) deep round cake tins.

Sift all the dry ingredients together three times (except sugar).

Wipe the inside of a metal mixing bowl with vinegar and dry (this is to remove any traces of grease, which will affect the egg whites). Beat the egg white until stiff and then quickly pour in the sugar while beating. Beat in the egg yolks on low. Stop when they are just combined. Gently fold through the dry ingredients.

Split the mix between the two cake tins and place in the middle of the oven. Bake for 24 minutes – but keep your eye on them as the cooking time nears completion. Test by gently pressing down on the centre of the cake – it should spring back. The sides of the cake should also have shrunk away from the side of the tin.

Remove from the oven and place in a draught-free place. Let them rest for 5 minutes before turning out onto a cooling rack covered with a tea towel (this stops the cake from being marked by the lines of the cooling rack). Allow to cool completely.

Sponge cakes will keep for two months frozen if wrapped in plastic wrap and foil.

easy chocolate cake

Serves 16

I use wholemeal (whole-wheat) flour in this cake because it makes it deliciously chewy and good.

- 180 g (6½ oz) unsalted butter, chopped and at room temperature
- 345 g (12 oz/1½ cups) caster (superfine) sugar
- 3 eggs
- 335 g (12 oz/2¼ cups) wholemeal (whole-wheat) self-raising flour (or 335 g whole-wheat flour with 2¼ teaspoons salt and 4½ teaspoons baking soda)
- 125 g (4½ oz/1 cup) Dutch (unsweetened) cocoa powder
- 375 ml (12½ fl oz/1½ cup) full-cream (whole) milk
- 3 teaspoons white vinegar
- 185 ml (6 fl oz/¾ cup) hot water

Preheat oven to 160°C (320°F). Grease and line a 23 cm (9 in) round cake tin with baking paper (parchment).

Throw everything together in a large bowl. Beat slowly until it starts to mix, then beat faster. Beat for around 5 minutes – the batter will lighten in colour as you beat.

Pour into the prepared tin and bake in the preheated oven for around 80–90 minutes, until a skewer inserted in the middle comes out clean. Allow to cool before turning out onto a cooling rack.

Once cool, cut the top off with a long serrated knife to create a flat top (if required). You can store in the refrigerator in an airtight container for a few days or freeze wrapped in plastic wrap and foil for up to two months.

basic butter cake

Serves 8

- 125 g (4½ oz) unsalted butter, at room temperature
- 1 teaspoon vanilla extract
- 170 g (6 oz/¾ cup) caster (superfine) sugar
- 2 eggs
- 225 g (8 oz/1½ cups) self-raising flour, sifted (or 225 g all-purpose flour with 1½ teaspoons of salt and 3 teaspoons of baking soda)
- 125 ml (4 fl oz/½ cup) full-cream (whole) milk

Preheat oven to 180°C (350°F). Grease and line a 20 cm x 5 cm (8 in x 2 in) deep round cake tin with baking paper (parchment).

Beat the butter, vanilla and caster sugar in a bowl until light and fluffy. Beat in the eggs. Stir in half the flour, then half the milk. Repeat. Add any colourings or flavours before pouring into the prepared pan.

Bake for 45–50 minutes, until a skewer inserted in the middle comes out clean. Allow to cool for 10 minutes before turning out onto a cooling rack topped with baking paper.

Once cool, you can store in the refrigerator in an airtight container for a few days or freeze for up to two months.

red velvet cake

Serves 16

This quantity makes two cakes.

- 345 g (12 oz/3 cups) cake flour (look for this on your supermarket shelf)
- 1 teaspoon bicarbonate of soda (baking soda)
- 2 tablespoons Dutch cocoa (unsweetened) powder
- ½ teaspoon salt
- 115 g (4 oz) unsalted butter, at room temperature
- 400 g (14 oz/1¾ cups) white sugar
- 250 ml (8½ fl oz/1 cup) vegetable oil
- 4 large eggs, separated and at room temperature
- 1 tablespoon vanilla extract
- 1 teaspoon white vinegar
- red gel paste food colour
- 250 ml (8½ fl oz/1 cup) buttermilk, at room temperature

Preheat oven to 170°C (340°F). Grease two 20 cm x 5 cm (8 in x 2 in) deep round cake tins and line with baking (parchment) paper, making a 3 cm (2 in) collar above the tin.

In a large bowl, sift the flour, bicarbonate of soda, cocoa powder and salt.

In another bowl beat the butter until smooth and creamy. Add the sugar and beat. Slowly pour in the oil while beating and continue to beat for around 2 minutes. Now beat in the egg yolks and vanilla, then the vinegar and, finally, the red food paste. Go slowly with the food colour – add and mix until you are happy with the shade.

Time to beat in the dry ingredients. Slowly beat in a third of the dry, then half the buttermilk, the next third dry, the remaining buttermilk, the remaining dry. Beat until just combined (don't overmix).

Beat the egg whites until they have soft peaks. Dollop a big spoonful of egg white onto the batter and mix in – this will lighten the overall mixture. Gently fold in the remaining whites until just combined.

Pour the batter evenly into the two cake tins. Now – don't skip this step: to keep the sides from browning whilst cooking, wrap a wet tea towel (dish towel) around the sides of the baking tin and then cover that with foil.

Bake for 40–45 minutes, or until a skewer inserted into the centre of the cake comes out clean.

Allow the cakes to cool completely on wire racks before turning out.

pound cake for a ball cake tin

Serves 8

- 250 g (9 oz) butter, at room temperature
- 230 g (8 oz/1 cup) caster (superfine) sugar
- 2 teaspoons vanilla extract
- 4 eggs
- 300 g (10½ oz/2 cups) plain (all-purpose) flour, sifted
- ½ teaspoon salt
- ½ teaspoon baking powder

Preheat oven to 160°C (320°F).

Prepare a 20 cm (8 in) ball cake tin by greasing it liberally with butter and then sifting flour onto it until it is completely dusted. To ensure that the cake cooks evenly – you don't want it to be brown on the outside and raw in the middle – wrap the tin in a wet tea towel (dish towel), then wrap that inside foil and place the whole thing inside a larger baking tin on a baking tray to keep it nice and level.

Beat the butter until it is as white as possible, then beat in the sugar and vanilla. Beat in the eggs one at a time until just combined. Sift the dry ingredients together in another bowl. Stir the flour, salt and baking powder through the batter until just combined (don't overwork the batter).

Now spoon the batter into the prepared tin and place in the middle of your oven. Bake for 75 minutes, or until a skewer inserted in the middle comes out clean (hold the skewer in the cake for a few seconds). Let it cool completely before turning out.

You can refrigerate or freeze the cake until you are ready to ice.

basic cookie recipe

Makes approximately 20

- 90 g (3 oz) unsalted butter (cold), diced
- 250 g (9 oz/1⅔ cups) plain (all-purpose) flour
- 85 g (3 oz/⅔ cup) icing (confectioners') sugar, sifted
- 1 egg, lightly whisked
- 1 teaspoon vanilla extract
- a pinch of salt

Mix cold butter and flour in a food processor until it is crumbly – don't overmix.

Put the butter mixture into a large mixing bowl, then add the icing sugar, egg, vanilla and salt. Mix with a spatula until smooth. Flatten the cookie mixture into a large oval and wrap with plastic wrap. Pop in the refrigerator to cool for 30 minutes.

When ready, shape your cookies how you want them, then lay them out on a baking tray lined with baking paper (parchment) and put in the freezer for 30 minutes to chill.

Preheat the oven to 180°C (350°F).

When the dough is chilled, bake for 18–20 minutes, until slightly golden.

bunny

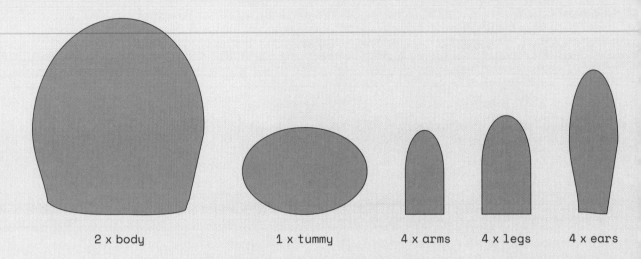

2 x body   1 x tummy   4 x arms   4 x legs   4 x ears

bat

little kitty friend

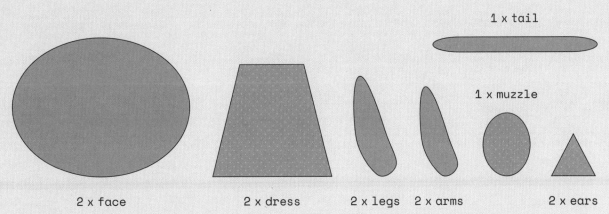

1 x tail

1 x muzzle

2 x face   2 x dress   2 x legs   2 x arms   2 x ears

cloud friend

flower shapes (not to scale)

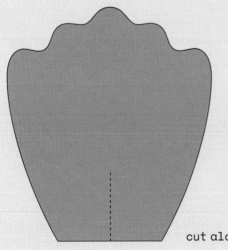

cut along dotted line

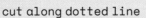

moustaches

dinosaur socks spikes

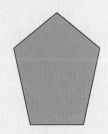

bookmark

fold along the dotted lines

felt fish

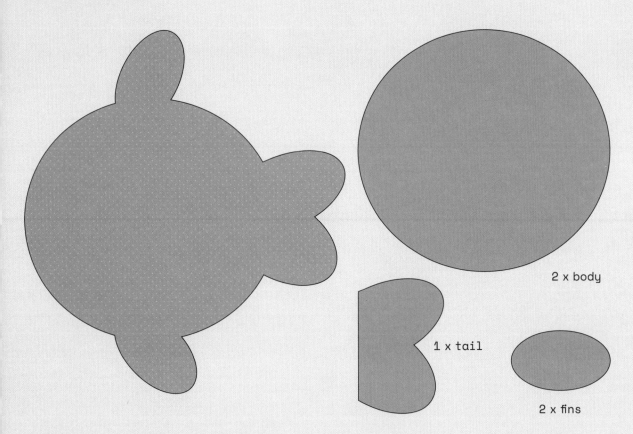

2 x body

1 x tail

2 x fins

rooster

about the author

Martine is a long-time crafter and hobbyist. She lives in Melbourne with her husband, two children, two cats, two rabbits and four hens. When she's not tending her ramshackle garden, making pompoms or wrangling children, she works as a freelance editor and writer.

thank you

Thanks to Tiffany Chua, who created the original felt fish friend and let me use her design. Brittany Watson Jepsen gave permission to use her cardboard cactus design. If you haven't discovered her website (thehousethatlarsbuilt.com) yet, check it out. Lyndsay Sung/Coco Cake Land (cococakeland.com) allowed me to use her design for the blue bear cake in the Teddy Bears' Picnic.

Pretty Wild (prettywild.com.au) generously loaned us their gorgeous dresses for the photo shoots and Seed (seedheritage.com) provided the pyjamas the girls wore in the Pancakes & Pyjamas party. Many thanks to Mel and Caroline at SleepoversRus (sleepoversrus.com.au) for the loan of the glamping tents – the children would have happily slept in those tents forever.

Thanks to Tahli Batkilin at Tahli's Treats (tahlistreats.com.au) for making the farm cupcakes for the Farm party and for sharing her recipe with us. Tahli's baking advice was much appreciated. Adam at Dahlia Fandango (www.dahliafandango.com) offered lots of great advice about edible flowers and sourced the most divine flowers for the photo shoots.

Many thanks to: Eleri Stephens for making the lovely garden tea party favour bags and helping with the girls' hair for the Garden Tea Party; Rebecca Pohlner for making the super cute bunny for pin the tail on the bunny and blackboard backdrop for the Science party; Harriet Oxley for costume advice and lending me some splendid pirate outfits; Rebecca Garcia Lucas for lending me her impressive toy collection; Erynn Moser for letting me borrow lots of pretty bibs and bobs; Natalie Lleonart for playing with cardboard boxes with me, lending me some very cool stuff and styling advice; and Mum for babysitting while I worked.

Thanks to all the children (and their parents) who came to the photoshoots: Alika, Argus, Aris, Astrid, Baillie, Belle, Billie, Charlotte, Elsie, Eva, Evie, Faizan, Freya, Isaac, Jasmine, Javan, Jenny, Kristian, Leni, Leo, Leonard, Max, Noah, Olivia, Ora, Orson, Persephone, Rosa, Rosie, Sasha, Spencer, Theo, Veronica and Ziggy.

At Hardie Grant, thanks to: Melissa Kayser for commissioning me and letting me run with it; awesome Anna Collett for her super organisation and enthusiasm and putting in long hours to get things on track (and a special thanks to Anna's mum & sister, who took time out of their holiday to come and help out at the first photo shoot); and Mark Campbell (a.k.a. Fix-it Fox) for setting things on their rightful course!

Antoana Oreski created the beautiful illustrations for the book and Sinéad Murphy put everything together in a lovely design. Thanks to Margaret Barca for a close, careful edit.

Thanks to Lauren Bamford – photographer extraordinaire, DJ and discerning tea drinker – for making everything look amazing and to Jacinta Moore – styling queen – for stepping in at the last minute and making everything so much easier. You guys are the best!

A big call-out to Greta Lleonart and Rebecca Pohlner who stepped in to help with food prep and styling for the photo shoots, along with making many cups of tea and generally helping things to run smoothly.

I couldn't have made this book without Rosa and Ikey – my expert resident consultants on all aspects of party planning.

Lastly, a huge thanks to Simon, who frequented op shops and dove into dumpsters to source props for the book; tested cakes (to the detriment of his waistline); put up with a hoard of children in his house during the photo shoots and assisted in innumerable other ways.

Published in 2017 by Hardie Grant Books,
an imprint of Hardie Grant Publishing

Hardie Grant Books (Melbourne)
Building 1, 658 Church Street
Richmond, Victoria 3121
hardiegrantbooks.com.au

Hardie Grant Books (London)
5th & 6th Floors
52–54 Southwark Street
London SE1 1UN
hardiegrantbooks.co.uk

A Cataloguing-in-Publication entry is available from the catalogue of the
National Library of Australia at www.nla.gov.au

Let's Party
ISBN 978 1 74117 528 8

Commissioning Editor: Melissa Kayser
Managing Editor: Marg Bowman
Project Editor: Anna Collett
Editor: Margaret Barca
Design Manager: Mark Campbell
Designer: Sinéad Murphy
Illustrator: Antoana Oreski
Photographer: Lauren Bamford
Stylist: Jacinta Moore
Proofreader: Kate Daniel
Production Manager: Todd Rechner
Production Coordinator: Rebecca Bryson

Colour reproduction by Splitting Image Colour Studio
Printed in China by 1010 Printing International Limited